Maximum Marriage

*In this revised and updated edition of Maximum Marriage,
Tim Timmons offers you the same wise, encouraging
counsel that he offers thousands in his marriage seminars
each year. You'll enjoy his unique suggestions and refreshing perspective on the role of the husband and wife. He
understands your problems and his advice will allow each
of you both individual and shared fulfillment. Let Tim
Timmons point you towards a maximum marriage that's
suited to the needs of life in the 1980's. He offers you:*

* *Fifteen dimensions of love found in I Corinthians 13*
* *Clarification of three misconceptions surrounding
  submission*
* *A sensitive guide to lovemaking from the Song of
  Solomon*
and much, much more

MAXIMUM MARRIAGE

TIM TIMMONS

Fleming H. Revell Company

Old Tappan, New Jersey

Scripture quotations in this volume are from the New American Standard Bible, © The Lockman Foundation 1960, 1962, 1963, 1968, 1971, 1972, 1973, 1975, 1977.

Chapter 5 is taken from Tim Timmons' book STRESS IN THE FAMILY, Copyright © 1982, Harvest House Publishers, 1075 Arrowsmith, Eugene, Oregon 97402. Used by permission.

Chapter 8 is taken from Tim Timmons' book LONELINESS IS NOT A DISEASE, Copyright © 1981, Harvest House Publishers, 1075 Arrowsmith, Eugene, Oregon 97402. Used by permission.

Library of Congress Cataloging in Publication Data

Timmons, Tim.
   Maximum marriage.

   Includes bibliographical references.
   1. Marriage—Religious aspects—Christianity.
I. Title.
BV835.T55 1983   646.7′8   82–19562
ISBN 0–8007–5106–X (pbk.)

TO Don and Sally Meredith, whose marriage was the original laboratory for many of these marital insights

TO thousands of couples who have invited me into their marriages through the medium of counseling

A special thanks to

Judith Ann Wilson for editing and coordinating the entire revision project

Craig and Ellen Parton for helpful editorial and research assistance

Tim Downs for his creative cartoons

Contents

Foreword

All weddings are happy; it's the living together afterward that causes the trouble. When the sparkle and glamour of that beautiful day wear off, a period of living together begins. Marriage has been described as a three-ring circus: first you have the engagement *ring,* then comes the wedding *ring,* and finally you get suffe*ring!* Others say that marriage is an adventure—like going off to war. Then there are those encouraging individuals who inform us that if it weren't for marriage, husbands and wives would have to fight with strangers!

You just can't find a successful game plan for marriage. There are all kinds of plans that equip you to argue fairly or divorce creatively. There are even plans that encourage you to include extramarital affairs in your marriage. Even though this gets a little crowded, it's a very popular plan. No doubt about it, there are a lot of exciting plans. The only problem is that they don't work.

You must have a game plan for marriage that works. A maximum marriage is where two individuals come together into a dynamic, intimate oneness, and through that oneness each enjoys a fulfillment of his or her individual life. A maximum marriage is found in the equation $1 + 1 = 1$. That is not new math. It is the only plan for marriage that works.

Something that is even more tragic than today's divorce rate is the incredible number of so-called marriages that are nothing more than living divorces! These homes are full of disappointment, resentment, and a spirit of enduring rather than enjoying marriage. It isn't that neither of the partners wants to make things work out for the best in the marriage relationship. But as each one seeks fulfillment and full expression of himself or herself, he meets with failure and disappointment. So it's time to give up. Then the man and the woman find themselves caught up in a marriage where all of their expectations for happiness are disintegrating before them. This process of disintegration is what I call Plan A.

Plan A

Plan A is by far the most popular plan for marriages today. It follows the familiar advice that "it'll all work out." Unfortunately, it is the way that it all works out that causes all the problems!

Plan A is based upon competition and comparison and constantly asks the question, "Who is more qualified, the man or the woman?" Thrilling things are happening in this home as each person sets out to answer this question by proving to be more qualified than the other. A real power struggle results and the Plan A marriage moves down the road to disappointment, resentment, and despair. Plan A does not work, yet most homes are operating on it! In order to capture a full description of the operation of Plan A, let's take a look at each family member in the process of disintegration.

Man

1. *Reasons from confusion.*   The man has heard the rumor that he is expected to be the *head* of his home. Since he never got a definition of that word, he begins to ask himself the question, "Who is more qualified?" Unfortunately, he comes up with two answers. His first obvious answer is, "Well, I am, of course!" But then he remembers the night before when he arrived home exhausted and felt like committing assault and battery on the kids after only eight minutes. Then he reflects on how his wife actually survives this type of pressure all day long. "Maybe she *is* more qualified than I

am." But he keeps hearing that same rumor that he should be the strong and powerful one in his home, so he feels the need to let all present know that he *is* the "head of the house." But his wife doesn't believe him—nobody else in the home votes for him—so he retreats. But the rumor is so prevalent that he takes six months off to research this word and comes back announcing, "I *am* the head . . . aren't I? *Can* I be, maybe from 6:00 to 7:30 P.M.—would that be all right? How about when you are out shopping, could I be the head *then?*" Confusion reigns, since the man does not know what his responsibility *is* in the home!

2. *Retreats from responsibility.*   Without a clear understanding of how he is to function within the framework of the home, the man retreats from his responsibility. His normal theme song goes something like this: "Honey, I'll take care of the office. You take care of the home. I will deposit. You will withdraw. If I can deposit more than you can withdraw or quicker than you can withdraw, then we will have a dynamic marital experience!" The most incredible thing is that the woman buys this proposition.

3. *Resents his wife.*   Once the man removes himself from active responsibility within the home, he sits back in the critic's chair. From his vantage point, resentment builds toward his wife for taking over in various family matters and decisions. The man who initially retreated from his responsibility is now filled with resentment toward his wife.

4. *Reacts against his wife.*   The resentment the man has for his wife surfaces in frequent confrontations as he tries to prove himself more qualified than his mate by pointing out where she's blown it. Usually he'll say, "If you had only consulted me, this problem would never have come up! Did you think to ask me before you did that? *Have you had a thought lately?*" He begins to erect a mental scoreboard and is sure to never let his wife slip ahead. He is really not interested in winning—he'll settle for a tie. This kind of reaction is nothing more than the deadlock of competition and comparison found within Plan A.

5. *Runs elsewhere.*   He's seeking fulfillment and full expres-

sion of himself as a person but hasn't found it at home, so he runs elsewhere. Often the man will marry his business. At least there he finds a thread of respect, appreciation, and full expression of himself. Since this guy is looking for involvement in anything other than his wife and home (he feels he has tried all that and failed), he may try some kind of sport (tennis, golf, hunting) or social organization (clubs, men's groups). He might even run to another woman—one who will truly listen to him and build him up. He'll run anywhere but home!

Woman

1. *Reasons from pride.*   The woman follows the same pattern as the man. Instead of starting from confusion, she begins from pride. After all, in her mind, being a wife can easily lead to being a doormat. Because of this misunderstanding of her function in the home, she is out to prove herself more qualified than a doormat. So when she asks herself the question, "Who is more qualified, the man or the woman?" her natural response is: "Well, I am, in many areas." *Besides,* she thinks, *If I don't do the work around here, it will never get done!* She's out to prove herself more qualified than a doormat, while her husband is trying to prove that *he* is the head. It's an exciting situation!

2. *Releases her husband from responsibility.*   In her energetic effort to outdo her husband and prove herself, she subconsciously pushes her husband out of meaningful involvement in the affairs of the home. She doesn't want to encourage him to take care of his responsibilities because she is out to show her husband that she is more qualified than he on the domestic front.

3. *Resents her husband.*   Although she has released her husband from his responsibility in the home, she begins to feel resentment toward him. She comes to the realization that she did not get a very good deal in the Plan A arrangement of the home. The woman is weighed down with the pressures of coordinating the activities of the home, the discipline of the children, the cooking of

the meals, and the cleaning of the house. In many ways she becomes a glorified taxicab driver! All kinds of pressures are on this woman, and she begins to wonder, *Where is that husband of mine?* On top of all this incredible amount of unappreciated work, she discovers that she is desperately lonely! She begins to resent her husband and his thoughts, opinions, and activities.

4. *Reacts against her husband.* She, too, begins to lash out against her mate because of her resentment of him. The familiar reaction is, "Where have you *ever* been when I needed you? When I need you you're never here! When I don't need you, there you are!" The atmosphere in the Plan A home at this point is pressure packed!

5. *Runs elsewhere.* She's seeking fulfillment and full expression of herself as a person, but hasn't found it at home. So *she* runs elsewhere. The woman normally will run to her children, hiding herself in a relationship with them that is only temporary. Soon the children grow up and are independent of Mom and Dad, and the woman must search for a relationship elsewhere. This time she may try women's organizations or a vocation. There is nothing wrong with any of these pursuits in themselves, but they are devastating when they are a replacement for a woman's relationship with her husband. Some women run toward other men, hoping to find someone who will care for them and treat them as valuable human beings.

Do you see what is happening in the Plan A home? Nobody's home! You can phone night and day, but no one will answer. Everyone is running away, looking for a relationship that seems impossible at home! This sets up one of the most tragic scenes in our society today—the development of the child within a Plan A home.

Child

1. *Reasons from insecurity.* The child's basic security factor is not derived from the fact that his mother and father love him but that his mother and father are excited about each other. The only problem is that within the Plan A home the parents just don't have

this kind of relationship. Instead of receiving security from his parents, he, too, is caught up in the pervasive spirit of competition and comparison within the home!

2. *Refuses to communicate.*   There is a natural shift in the development of a child from dependence to independence. In order to survive this shift with relatively few explosions, the parent-child relationship must be healthy and warm. Within the Plan A home, though, this shift is met with a cold system of rules. The child responds to this system by retreating in order to create and live in a world all his own which excludes his parents. Parent-child communication suffers and "heavy, gut-level" conversation such as, "If you're not in by eleven we're padlocking your stereo" or "Can I have the car tonight?" becomes the norm. The *real child*, with his interests, thoughts, and feelings, gradually becomes the concealed child. At least he is unknown to his parents!

3. *Resents his parents.*   By this time, the child experiences enough of Plan A through observing his parents, and he joins the power struggle. The parents respond with more and more restrictions, but restrictions without a relationship cause rebellion every time. Now he's out to prove something. "I'm not too young! I know what I'm doing!"

A mother asked me, concerning her fourteen-year-old son, "What can I do about my *baby?* He's been so rebellious lately." It didn't take a lot of insight to discern the problem. I responded, "You might begin by dropping *baby* from your vocabulary."

"Oh, but he's our *baby.*" On his sixteenth birthday the *baby* obtained his driver's license, took the car out on his first solo drive, and returned home drunk. Obviously he was sending a message: "I'm not a baby!"

4. *Runs elsewhere.*   The child was meant to find fulfillment and full expression of himself as a person within the family unit. Instead, he (just like mom and dad) must search outside the home. He finds himself at the mercy of his peers. It's at this point the child is surrounded by strong social and emotional pressures to experiment or try different things for acceptance. These experiences can

be unhealthy, defeating, and sometimes damaging for the child because he has no secure base from which to step out into the world.

One of the most tragic effects upon children in the Plan A home is the problem of homosexuality. In a book highly endorsed by the National Institutes of Health entitled *Growing Up Straight*, Peter Wyden reveals:

> Research findings overwhelmingly indicate that homosexuals are not born but bred . . . there is increasing agreement that homosexuals rarely (if ever) occur without some important (or controlling) contribution from parents. . . . Many parents underestimate their own importance as models for the behavior of their children, especially while the children are still young. . . . They should appreciate that a mother's acceptance of her role as a truly feminine woman will communicate itself to a daughter at a remarkably early age; and that a mother's respect for the father's role as the man of the family will help a small boy grow up to be masculine. On the other hand, if parents themselves are unsure about what constitutes appropriate male and female behavior today—or, especially, if they are competitive with each other [Plan A]—their children are bound to become confused about their place in the scheme of things.

Study after study shows that the Plan A home is producing a high-risk child, one vulnerable to every sickness society has to offer. He is vulnerable to the drug scene, to promiscuity, to just about anything floating around in our society that looks worth running after. Most important, the Plan A child is a high-risk child in the area of his own identity. He just doesn't know who he is, and once he finds out, it seems worse!

The Plan A child has lost a secure base from which to step out into the world, and his parents, for all practical purposes, have lost their child.

Not only does the Plan A home not work but it's also empty, as everyone wanders about searching for relationships they can't find at home.

Plan B

What we need is a plan of hope for living together in marital oneness: a plan for maximum marriage. Plan B is a game plan for marriage which provides for fulfillment and full expression for the man and the woman as individuals and as partners with a dynamic oneness of the marital relationship. This plan is not based on competition but on completeness: two people completing one another in oneness. *Maximum Marriage* sets forth the definition, operational principles, and illustrations of Plan B.

The Oneness Factor

The first ingredient of a Plan B marriage is the *oneness factor.* Perhaps the best illustration of this key principle is found in the Book of Genesis in the Bible. In this book you have God creating all kinds of wild things. God creates the earth and says, *It's good!* He creates plants and says, *It's good!* He creates animals and again says, *It's good!* Then God creates Adam, takes one good look at him and says, *This is not good!* You can just hear Adam saying, "Who, me?"

God says, *Right. You, Adam. You're alone. You're incomplete.* Here's Adam, with everything a guy could hope for—a good employer, super retirement benefits, great food, perfect accommodations, no crabgrass in the front lawn, even a perfect relationship with God. Still God says, *Nope. Sorry, Adam, but you just are not complete. You need someone to complete you.*

At this point in the story God does one of the strangest things I've ever read in my life. He brings all of the animals to Adam so that Adam can pick out his completor. Now Adam doesn't know any better. He's never seen a woman before. So we have Adam checking out the animals in order to find one suitable for him. Can you imagine what must be going on out there? First God brings Adam a giraffe, and you can just hear him saying, "No! That is just not what I had in mind at all." Next, an elephant plops by. Adam begins to panic. "Please, God, no! Can't we negotiate something a little different?" Through this bizarre process God develops in Adam a great sense of appreciation for the future Eve. Furthermore, if God hadn't taken Adam through this process, Adam could have come back after his first squabble with Eve and said, "Listen, God, how about a giraffe? I mean, *anything* would be better than this!"

Then God creates Eve and brings her to Adam, and this guy goes berserk! He just goes wild right there before God, the animals, and all of creation! Adam blurts out, "This is now bone of my bones and flesh of my flesh. She shall be called woman because she was taken out of man." Does that sound as though he is excited? No. Unfortunately, the King James Version of the Bible miswords a few parts. This is one of those parts. The phrase, "this is now" is a terrible way of expressing what Adam is doing at this point. The Hebrew word here means "Wow!" Adam went bananas! He started whistling and jumping up and down. His response said, "Wrap her up. I'll take her. On second thought, don't wrap her up. I'll take her just as she is!" The same thing happened when you met the man or woman you were going to marry—Wow!

A young man walked into our apartment one day without even knocking. He just walked in and said, "I met *her.*" I said, "What?" He said, "I met *her.*" I said, "Who?" He said, *"Her."* I had to get him a glass of water and settle him down—he was a basket case. That guy had just experienced a Wow. The Wow of the wedding day and thrill of the honeymoon, and all of a sudden that Wow turns into *ugh....*

How do you put the Wow back into your marriage? I was rocking along in my marriage for the first three years. I was shooting at my wife, slicing away at her, never realizing that I needed to view her as my completor. She was my only hope for life—not my obstacle in life. Once I began to see her as my complement and not my competition, our marriage began to change like you would not believe. As a matter of fact, my wife was so suspicious of me for the first two months after my attempt to change from being a clod to trying to do a few things right in our marriage that she thought I had either filed for divorce or was seeing another woman. I distinctly remember saying something very nice to her one day. She looked at me and asked, "Why are you doing this?"

All of us need a good dose of Wow in our marriages. In Part I you'll learn how to put the Wow back into your marriage!

The Responsibility Factor

The second principle of a maximum marriage (Plan B) is the *responsibility factor*. Here we're talking about the man's responsibility and the woman's responsibility. In Part II we will tackle the idea of the husband as head in the home. I said *head*, not dictator! And we'll look at the idea of the woman's responsibility in the home and how she differs from a doormat!

One of the major factors behind the comparison and competition with Plan A is the gross misunderstanding of the responsibilities of the husband and wife. It is because of this misunderstanding that the man has truly trampled the woman under his feet. Even with this "kingly" or dictatorial position, he finds an uncertainty of his identity in the home and an ache of aloneness.

The man shouldn't take all the blame. The woman may be gently but steadily nudging him out of the house by emasculating her man. Now she's in charge, only to find herself overwhelmed by pressures and left very much alone to cope with life.

A proper understanding of these responsibilities and how they interrelate offers an essential ingredient to a maximum marriage—two fulfilled and fully expressed individuals drawing strength from their marital oneness.

The Intimacy Factor

The third principle in a maximum marriage is the *intimacy factor*. When we talk about intimacy we are really talking about communication. This is where the nitty gets gritty. There are two dimensions of intimacy: spiritual and physical. Spiritual intimacy has to do with your nonverbal communication. There are certain things about your mate's spirit that just tick you off, right? Maybe it's the *way* he says something or the *way* he rolls his eyes. I purse my lips in a certain way when I'm upset. When I do that my wife immediately says, "Aha, you're doing that to your lips again." The way we express our spirits and our moods is critical in building or breaking a marriage.

Take the husband who comes home in the evening and asks, "Where's dinner?" But he says it in a way that communicates so much more than that. He asks, "Where's dinner?" but his spirit says, *What in the world have you been doing all day that dinner is not here on the table?*

His wife says, "What do you mean, where's dinner?" but her spirit is saying, *What do you mean, what have I been doing all day, you dodo!* When confronted with the spirit of his communication he says, in all innocence, "All I said was, 'Where's dinner?'" But that's not all he said. He said *so* much more!

The most intimate and sensitive area of all is physical communication—sex. For years, studies have indicated that finances and sex are the two major causes of divorce. Although these are definite, common problem areas, they are also symptoms of the health or illness of the marital relationship. Sex serves as a marital barometer of what's going on in the intimate dynamics of the marital communication system. Therefore, we will examine the underlying principles of physical communication so that a healthy expression of a maximum marriage can be experienced!

The Supernatural Factor

The fourth crucial principle in a maximum marriage is the *supernatural factor.*

A man came into my office one day and said, "My wife is a zero." I said, "A what?"

"A zero," he responded. "Well," I replied, "What's that?"

He said, "Would minus help?" I said, "Yes, that helps a little bit."

He went on. "She just can't do anything."

"What about you?" I asked.

"Well," he said, "I'm in a heap of trouble, you understand, but she's a zero." He kept talking until finally he just blurted it out: "You know, what we need is to turn completely inside out."

"I've got something for you," I replied. "You need something down here at the gut level."

Change at the gut level of our beings. There is a supernatural dimension of our beings through which we can experience positive change. The supernatural factor is not mysterious, spooky, weird, or even a "religious experience." Miraculous changes occur for those willing to try it.

Principles of life are true no matter what you think or believe about them. They're like the laws of nature. For instance, there is the principle of gravity. Stated simply, this principle says if you jump off a two-story building, you'll come down fast and hit with a thud. And you probably won't like it! It doesn't make any difference what you think or believe—or whether or not you like it. The principle is true. Even if the principle of gravity were placed on a national ballot and voted down unanimously, the next person who attempted to jump off a two-story building would find that the principle didn't know it had been voted out of existence. As he jumped, he would come down fast and hit with a thud. And he probably wouldn't like it!

When you follow the principles of life, you'll experience personal fulfillment. If you ignore these principles, you'll experience everything *but* personal fulfillment.

You don't have to understand life's principles to follow them. I don't understand how electricity works, but I flip the switch and read by the light. I don't understand how a brown cow can eat green grass and make white milk and yellow butter, but I eat all of it—except the grass! Principles are true no matter what level of understanding you have of them.

The principles of life can govern your life toward maximum fulfillment of who you are! There are principles of life-style that relate to you alone, to you and your relationships, and to you and your vocation. These principles of life are vital in understanding how a marriage works.

After much searching, I have found that one Book contains these vital principles of life. (It's not one of mine.) Let me give you the title. It's the Bible! Oh, not the Hoooly Bible—just the Bible! Now before you panic, let me explain what I mean.

On a flight from New York to Los Angeles, an executive sat down next to me. After a few conversational clichés, he asked, "What do you do?" I quickly replied, "I speak."

He said, "I know that, but what do you do for a living?" Again I said, "I speak!"

"On what?" he continued. "Well, I speak on life-style, marriage, parenting, long-term selling and managing, and such."

He seemed interested. "Really! Are you a psychiatrist?"

"No," I replied, "but I have a psychiatrist who works with me."

"Well, then," he said, "are you a psychologist?"

"No, I'm not one of those, either, but I do have two of them who work for me."

Then, in a somewhat frustrated manner he asked, "Well, what are you?" Now it hurts a little bit when someone asks, "What are you?" but I bounced back with, "I'm just a speaker!" Now that my profession was established, he started on his second set of twenty questions!

"Where do you get your material?" I told him he probably wouldn't believe me if I told him. "No," he said, "come on, where do you get your stuff?" So I told him, "I get it out of a Book."

"In a book! What's the title of the book?" he asked. I had him get out his pen. He fumbled for a minute and finally got his pen and datebook in hand to receive the title of my resource Book. Calmly I announced, "The title of the Book is the Bible."

He seemed a little stunned by my answer and said in a rather loud voice, "Bible? You get your material to speak to corporations from the Bible? What is there to talk about in the Bible?"

I'd heard that question so many times in similar situations, I was ready for it. "Oh," I said, "I speak quite a bit on sex!"

He choked slightly. "From the Bible?" His shock came from a common misconception that the Bible says, "Thou shalt not!" about sex. It actually says, "Thou shalt!" and it even goes so far as to say, "Thou shalt enjoy it, when thou shalt!"

"Oh, yes, from the Bible!" I assured him. "There are all kinds of principles of life concerning sex in the Bible! Moses wrote in Deuteronomy 24:5 that when a man gets married, he shouldn't be drafted into the military or work, but he should cheer up his wife for a year! I can't explain it all right now, but that Hebrew word for 'cheer up' doesn't mean to tell jokes for a year. It's referring to sex!"

Now the inquisitive executive began to take notes. "Now, where is that verse?" Can't you just see him going to his hotel room and pulling out the Gideon Bible from the nightstand drawer! Principles of life are universal principles, and no matter where you find them, people want them. That's because they are true to people as they are and life as it is!

It's none of my business what you live by or what you think about the Bible. I feel like the automobile commercial that states, "If you can find a better car, buy it!" If you can find a better source for principles of life that are tuned to people as they are and life as it is, then you'd better buy it!

Part I

The Oneness Factor:
Competition or
Completion?

1

Wrap Her Up, I'll Take Her!

There are three stages of a marriage today. The first is the "ideal." Once this fantasy wears off, the ideal becomes the "ordeal." As the ordeal wears people down, most begin looking for a "new deal."

Marriages move in phases. Some couples consciously know they are moving through these phases, but most just know that their re-

lationship has changed. The first phase of the marital relationship is the "honeymooners." If we were to put this phase of marriage into an equation, I would simply call it $1 + 1 =$ who knows what? Two people who are excited about each other and, for the most part, oblivious to each other's faults. They have no game plan for marriage, but who cares, since their mutual love seems able to allow them to conquer any problem.

With time comes the second phase: the "roommates." The honeymoon is over and the desire to show every visitor the wedding pictures waned months ago. The marriage is now seen in a geographical way: "Yeah, we live together." The marital equation now reads $1 + 1 = 2$.

Phase three brings the "family." *Survival* is a key word at this point. Each partner is desperately hoping to find something that will make the marriage take off. Finally they get the answer: Babies! Since they seem to have so many problems between them and feel an increasing loss of oneness, they look for something that will bring back their former closeness. "A baby, yep, that will help us make this marriage work," they reason. The equation gets exciting because now they end up with $1 + 1 + 1 = 3$!

As the marriage begins to move into focus around the children, something very rude happens—the children grow up! After the kids are out of the house and off on their own, a painful reality sets in. The two people who began this whole program are now left alone with each other.

With phase four comes what I call the "business partners." Our original couple now goes looking for a new pizzazz, something that will fill the void that occurs once having children loses its glamour. The marriage is then reduced to two people trying to "find themselves." However, this desperate search for identity normally ends up in a frantic and lonely exhaustion. What started out as building a relationship toward oneness is now drifting apart into a cold separation, because everyone is out chasing himself!

Honeymoon Attacks

The weirdest things happen right in the middle of one of these phases. You might be into "family" but at the same time realize that you really ache for some excitement in your marital relationship. Then you remember the excitement each of you felt for each other during the honeymoon phase. You decide that you want to act like honeymooners again. Unfortunately you can never seem to pull off being honeymooners—either you're in the mood and he isn't, or he is and you're not! It's difficult to get it together! People become irritated at this point because they are sure the answer to their marital unrest is to go back to the honeymoon phase. Drifting and floating in the marriage begins as each partner magnetically searches for another potential honeymoon.

"Honeymoon attacks" are common in the "roommate" phase of a marriage. Each partner thinks, *What are we doing? All we share is geography. I live here. He lives here. That's it! We check in with each other occasionally to make sure all the vital signs are functioning, but we need more. We need something new.* For the craving honeymooner, any warm body will do. As long as everyone wants to play honeymooner (let's-get-to-know-each-other fantasy and no reality) it makes no difference what your name is.

Mid-Life "Heart" Attacks

Another very common attack against the marital relationship is the popularized mid-life crisis "heart" attack. This is an earthquake within the emotional structure of man and woman. The man has been charging and driving toward his goals (usually married to his business) as a workaholic. In mid-life he wakes up. He realizes that he has an emotionally painful ache of loneliness. He is basically bankrupt in human relationships, and probably will not reach his goals anyway. Others reach their goals but find an emptiness in their success because they had to mortgage their families in the process. In both cases, an emotional eruption occurs in which a man is driven toward the honeymooner phase with anyone who will play. He has been an all-work-and-no-play man, and therefore "Jack" has become a dull boy. So now he wants to *live* life to the fullest!

The woman also experiences an emotional "heart" attack. Whereas the man overdosed on work and performance, the woman overdoses on being needed. She's needed as a cook, a homemaker, a "taxicab" driver, a nurse, a neighbor, a lover, a volunteer, a calendar specialist, a daughter, an in-law, and so forth. Her emotional eruption is that she arrives at a point in life where the kids are gone and she's not needed as much as before. She was getting a little tired of all the strings attached to her life anyway. But now for survival she wants to do something for "me"!

Both of these people want a oneness that satisfies. Instead they have each found that oneness (as they defined it and acted it out) robbed them of satisfaction and their individual fulfillment.

After this poor experience in achieving oneness, most people throw out the concept of oneness altogether as impossible and undesirable. Yet the very thing each person needs in order to discover and experience self-fulfillment and real life together is a healthy concept of oneness. It's $1 + 1 = 1$! It's a game plan that makes life and marriage work!

Most marriages share two common scenes: reacting to weaknesses and building treadmills of performance.

Reacting to Weaknesses

I did a home-study series for couples a few years ago, and I tried something that I'll never try again. I opened up the first meeting full of strangers by saying, "Let's begin this series by telling the group what you think is the most endearing quality about your mate." There was absolute silence in the room. Finally a man in the back stood up and said, "I've never told my wife this, but I really appreciate her consistent loving spirit in the home. When I'm depressed she is able to lift my spirits up. She's fantastic." His wife's eyes welled up with tears. She searched for her handkerchief and ran off to the bathroom.

A woman then shared, "I don't think I've ever said this to my husband, but I love his sense of stability and confidence. He gives me so much security." Her husband, moved with emotion, looked down as if to hold back from crying. It was a very emotional time. The line to the bathroom just kept getting longer and longer! In nearly every case, each person who shared began with, "I haven't told my mate, but...." Why do most people neglect telling strengths to their mates? Why is it so easy to pick out the weaknesses?

To win in marriage you have to stop reacting to your mate's weaknesses and start receiving your mate, weaknesses and strengths included, as your completor, not as your competition.

Building Treadmills of Performance

Not only is it natural to focus on the other's weaknesses but it is also easy to place your mate on the treadmill of performance. There are two lists each person carries in his frontal lobe regarding a mate: *weaknesses* and *expectations*. For the most part, these lists originated before marriage, during the engagement period. It was then that the man and woman began to seek counsel concerning things each would like to change in his or her potential mate. Each possessed a list and sought advice from various neighborhood marriage counselors—Mother, Aunt Ruth, and the like. The advice was simple and optimistic: "It'll all work out!" The couple confidently approached the wedding day excited about life together.

After the thrill of the honeymoon wore off, each partner received a terrible shock. One fateful day each person came to the realization that the original lists of weaknesses were incomplete! Not only were there many more weaknesses that needed to be changed but the chances of changing those on the original lists appeared slim.

Very few of us consciously place our mates on a treadmill, but when closely examined we all encounter one another with many expectations. Almost everyone has a hidden agenda in relationships—the things we want or expect others to be and do. Even though it's not a conscious thought most of the time, it is very real—especially to those who work out on our treadmills.

Although few of us are aware of setting up treadmills for others, almost everybody recognizes the treadmills of performance laid just for them. When a person feels unknown by another, misunderstood, unheard, or boxed in, that person is working out on a treadmill of someone else's expectations.

Jerks Are Not Terminal

Weaknesses and expectations. Both of these are characterized by *competition,* which basically consists of each mate keeping score of what the other has done wrong as far as what he or she is expected to do. It's a thrills-and-chills situation! Even the normal marital quarrels reflect the score sheets that have been carefully recorded by each partner. No one really wants to win, but just to keep it even!

I asked one couple who had incorporated many innovations in quarreling (including throwing lamps) how a heated quarrel actually started. She said, "Well, it might start out by my reminding him of. . . ." He said, "Yes, and when she brings that up I remind her of her actions when she did. . . ."

"And when he drags that out, I remind him of the time. . . . " He said, "No, you don't. You tell me of the time I. . . ."

She said, "Oh, yes, that's right!" Do you see what happened? Each knew what the other was going to say and in the proper order. It was as if they each had their lists of weaknesses and expectations memorized. The only change was the length of the lists and the heat of the arguments.

I've often wondered why people don't tape their arguments. They're so similar. Think of the brilliant lines that have gone unrecorded or the decibel levels that will never be reached again. If we could have them all on tape, we'd only have to push a button when we got upset. Then each person would be free to make faces and create gestures toward the other. What an energy saver!

Competition gnaws away at the very foundation of the marriage union. I found my own marriage drifting away from the oneness we had first experienced. It was as if someone were driving a wedge between my wife and me. There was a growing distance between us. I felt alone, and that really bugged me.

When I returned from a speaking engagement in another part of the country, a friend of mine picked me up at the airport. He told me about a jerk he was counseling who was tearing up his marriage. As he explained what Mr. Jerk was doing to his wife, I realized I was related to the Jerk family in many ways.

I couldn't wait to get home and explain to my wife what a jerk I had been. I'd been shoving her out of my life and making her into someone I didn't even like! When I got home I said, "Honey, I've got to talk to you. I love you. I really need you. I've been rejecting you and slicing away at you. I'm sorry for what I've done." She looked at me and said, "That's fine." Then she got up and walked out of the room.

Something told me that she wasn't impressed, so I planted myself near the kitchen, knowing that she would have to move in that direction soon. She did. I took her by the arm and sat her down and went through my whole explanation again. She began to cry and I began to cry—it was a mess! But our marriage has never been the same since that day we decided to see each other as completors instead of competitors!

In order to view your mate as one who can perfectly complete you rather than compete with you, you must: (1) follow the pattern of Adam; (2) commit yourself to the basic principles of marriage; and (3) learn to enjoy the product.

Follow the Pattern of Adam

In Genesis 2 God told Adam the bad news and the good news. The bad news was that Adam was alone and that wasn't good. The good news for Adam was that God would make a helper suitable for him. The first "not good" in the Bible was used to describe Adam's aloneness.

Ache of Aloneness

Nothing is more painful than the ache of aloneness in a marriage. There is a great need in marriage to be able to share emotionally with each other. It's that ache that you feel when you can't wait for your husband to come home so that you can tell him about something exciting that has happened to you. He comes in, you drop it on him and he says, "Do I smell meat loaf again?" Or, you want to tell your wife about some exciting plans for your future and she says, "You sure dream a lot. The only problem is that most of your dreams turn out to be nightmares." There is a gnawing ache of aloneness in marriage. There is an intense need for emotional oneness!

Instead of standing together against trials, Plan A marriages become battlegrounds where each partner accuses the other of bringing problems into the marriage. Let's look in on a couple filled with the pain of being alone. "Jean and I got married three years ago when I was in my last year of engineering school. Now it seems as though we always have these picky problems that just bug me. For instance: she put me through school for a year; now she's worked two more years on top of that, so she wants to have a family *right now*. She's twenty-four and I'm twenty-six, but we can't have a family right now! And the reason we can't is that I need two more years to get us situated financially before I have the responsibility of children. She cannot understand what I need to do to get us prepared—*then* we can have a family."

So this is Carl; and now Jean, his wife of three years, says, "Carl, money is not more important than our happiness, and I do not want to wait until I'm twenty-six to have a baby."

Now here is a couple having some real problems. Their marriage is not on the verge of collapse, but things are not going as well for them as they would like. They're not experiencing what they were expecting from marriage.

There are other complaints: he feels she is too naggy about his clothes ... and the trash ... and fixing things around the apartment.

Jean says, "Well, I'm not a maid, am I? We both live here, and I shouldn't have to be the only one to lift a finger in the apartment and try to keep it clean. Don't forget, I've got a full-time job, too."

Carl responds, "Yes ... right ... and that job must be making you pretty tired, especially at night, when it's time to supposedly enjoy each other's company in bed. I don't know, I try to do my part to get something going ... but then you're too tired. That really motivates me. It motivates me so much that I'm getting a little disinterested myself. I wish I could count the times I've thought to myself during the day, *I wish she could show some interest in trying to enjoy sex. She always waits for me to get something going. For once, I wish she could take just a little bit of initiative.*"

Although in other areas many of their needs as persons are being met, they both sense that something is missing, and they both really want more than they're getting.

They handle a lot of situations well, but they're not close. They're not as close as they used to be before they got married, and they are not as close as they thought they'd be after they got married.

Jean says, "Somehow I just feel as if we don't even touch anymore. The gentleness and tenderness are just not there very often. I mean, I know we're both busy, but even when we are together and we try to talk, it just seems there's this invisible wall there between us, bouncing our words back at us. I feel as though we're together, we're in the same room, but we're not really *together*—we're *alone.*"

To the degree that your mate does not meet your needs, you *are* alone!

The ache of aloneness is no more apparent than in the divorce statistics. Any statistician can compute that if the current rate of divorce continues, we will have *no* husband-wife families in this country by the year 2008! Of even more concern are the living divorces that are a reality in countless homes. The ache of aloneness is an epidemic!

The place to begin in viewing your mate as your completor is to realize that, without your mate, *you are alone.* To follow the pattern of Adam is to realize that you need *your* mate to complete you.

Think about Adam for a minute. He knew that Eve had weaknesses when God brought her to him. He could easily have said, "Listen, God, while You're doing this creating business, this woman You gave me is a little chunky, so would you consider slimming her down?" Or maybe he could have said, "God, could I suggest a slight alteration to any future plans for making women? Put a contraption on her mouth with a button for control purposes. She talks way too much!" Why didn't Adam say anything about her weaknesses? I think he realized something that we don't—that to reject his mate in any way, shape, or form would be to blow the whole game plan for marriage. To reject her would be to close the door on the only hope he had for oneness.

To reject your mate is to reject your only hope for oneness and it will also be a major contributing factor in the process of disintegration.

2

Throw Away Your Fig Leaves

After following the pattern of Adam, you must commit yourself to three fundamental principles of marriage. The first principle is that you must *leave*. This is the idea of severance—not going back to Mommy and Daddy after you have established your own home and marriage. Many marriages have real problems because this principle is violated. Countless couples have committed to marriage but have never left home financially or emotionally. *Leaving* means to break one's dependence upon one's parents—it's an attitude, not necessarily a geographical change.

A woman expressing to me a series of heated arguments with her husband repeatedly referred to her mother. I asked, "Does your mother live with you?" She said, "Oh, no, she lives in Fort Worth [thirty-five miles away]."

"Well, then, how does she get involved in these arguments?"

"It's easy," she replied. "When we start fighting I call her up and she comes over." That *was* easy! Going back to Mommy cuts away at the oneness of the relationship.

The second fundamental principle of marriage is that of permanence—the need to *cleave*. To cleave to your mate is to be committed to permanence, to stick together like glue.

Divorce results when two people get tired of cleaving, or possi-

bly never cleaved together in the first place! They are tired of sticking it out, of tolerating the living hell in their home. A marriage must not be tolerated—it should be changed. Change can happen if two people are willing to work at their marriage. To stay in a marriage for the sake of financial security, children, or business is ridiculous. It's even more ridiculous to exit a marriage without attempting to change with the help of an effective third-party counselor. But to work to make the equation $1 + 1 = 1$ true of your marriage is worth it! Even if you feel you must have been in an altered state of consciousness when you chose your mate, you can still experience fulfillment, full expression of your individuality, and completeness in your marriage. A commitment to cleaving is the hope for your marriage.

The third principle is that of *intimacy*—the oneness that results from leaving and cleaving is to be expressed in a way that is free from inhibitions. Genesis says that the man and the woman were both naked and not ashamed.

Recently I was performing a wedding and an older gentleman was assisting me. As I read this portion from Genesis, the man started choking! He came up afterward and, looking very somber, said, "You know, we don't read that here."

"You don't read what?" I asked.

"Well," he said, "that passage where they're both standing there without any clothes on."

This man missed the whole point! This portion of the Bible is talking about two people who are totally open, emotionally and physically. That's intimacy, and that's what we've got to have if we're going to make marriage work.

Enjoying the Product

Get Free From Reaction

The results of committing yourself to the process of completion rather than competition are significant. First of all, *you are free from reacting to your mate's weaknesses.*

A lady who attended one of my seminars wrote the following:

You don't have to be married long to get the picture that you are linked up with a real live person who comes complete with a first-class set of weaknesses. During the days of dating they are unnoticed; during the early days of marriage they are overlooked; now, however, they are getting to be unbelievable! You know, it's one thing when he watches football games on the two-day honeymoon, but now, out of a total of twenty-three hours of football on the tube over Thanksgiving, he watches twenty-one hours. The other two hours he falls asleep on the sofa.

Here was a wife who was feeling a growing irritation and frustration because of weaknesses and faults in her husband. As an example of the situation they were involved in, it might be interesting to relive a typical day. Many wives will identify with this.

In the morning she gets up first to feed the children, while he catches an extra thirty minutes in the sack. So, right off the bat she resents him for being lazy. Under her breath she's saying to herself, "It's always *Daddy* when company is here, and *Mommy* when it's time for breakfast."

Finally, when he does fall out of bed, he makes a mad dash for his bath, scans the sports page while hastily eating breakfast, and then flashes by her as he jumps into his car and speeds off down the freeway to work.

Meanwhile, her problems have only just begun as she picks up the trail he has left behind him on his journey from the bed to the front door. Socks, underwear, wet towels, newspapers, and bathrobe clearly mark his path.

Once the path has been cleared, she is faced with overhauling the bathroom. First of all, she picks the soap out of the tub water where he has left it to get soft; then she drains and cleans the tub and hangs up his towel and washcloth. Not only is there water all over the side of the sink and on the floor where he has been shaving but it's also all over the mirror and walls. So she wipes all that off and puts away his razor, deodorant, toothbrush, toothpaste, comb, and hair spray, and finally unplugs his hot-lather machine.

Meanwhile, the children have completely demolished the living room, the day is half over, and she's beginning to realize that this guy she thought was her heartthrob is turning out to be a royal pain in the neck.

The day progresses; he's forty-five minutes late for dinner, comes home and gobbles down the meal she's worked on for three hours, then props himself on the sofa to laugh it up with Dandy Don and the rest of the boys on Monday-night football. Meanwhile, she's bathing and dressing the kids for bed, straightening up the house, and getting ready for Monday-night dishes. After all, what are women for? He takes care of the office, she takes care of the home.

Application of the principle? The day this woman commits herself to the principle of oneness is the day she begins to see these weak areas of her husband's life as opportunities of blessing for her. And ladies, if you can be blessed through football, then there is no limit to how you can be blessed.

Get Free From the Treadmill

When you see that the greatest goal in your marriage is to experience the oneness factor, you are released from the normal cutting response against your mate. You must view your mate's weaknesses for what they are—tools that can help fashion your marriage into one of completion instead of competition.

The second benefit of committing yourself to oneness is that *you are released from the performance treadmill.* It's only as you view your mate as your completor that you are able to take him or her off the performance treadmill. You no longer treat your mate as a competitor. When your mate feels totally accepted, the very atmosphere of acceptance and excitement encourages greater performance than ever.

A commitment to oneness will result in a change in your mate. One couple, whose marriage was filled with explosive "discussions," came to me seeking help. Their arguments normally climaxed in throwing things. He didn't seem too interested in talking to me, so I sent him into another room. I asked her, "When did all of this start?" She said, "Three months ago I realized that he rarely came home on time, so I set up a rule." I knew this was really going to be a winner. When I inquired about the rule, she rose to the occasion with a display of creative genius. "I told him that if he didn't come home at half-past five he couldn't eat!" She sat back with a satisfied grin.

How had her husband responded to this new rule? He hadn't come home at half-past five for the entire three months! I asked, "Would you say, on the basis of this three-month experiment, that your rule is working?" She laughed nervously, looked at me somewhat perplexed, and said, "I never thought of it that way."

This couple was trapped in competition and both of them were keeping score. She was saying, "I have the right for you to be home at a decent time in the evening!" That made the score 1-0. Not wanting to win, but just to keep the score even, he began to say, "Well, I have the right to stay out as late as I wish—and even eat better!" Now the score was 1-1!

I explained the concept of the oneness factor to her. The logical application of the principle was for her to revoke the rule. I told her, "Look, this is not going to work. Forget that crazy rule and go in that room and tell him you'll feed him royally no matter *when* he arrives home for dinner, but that you would like to see him home around half-past five."

That was a tough assignment for her, but she did it. Each night for the next two weeks, her husband came home at half-past five on the dot. One day, after realizing that I had had a part in his wife's actions, he called me at exactly half-past five and said, "I'm home!" and hung up. This wife saw a significant change in her husband's behavior through a commitment to the oneness factor.

Suggested Steps to Oneness

Notice that these are *suggested steps.* The application of these steps may vary from person to person and situation to situation. So you may take the following steps and throw them out, burn them, or you may embrace them as your own. But whatever you do, you must apply the principle of oneness, and begin to see your mate's weaknesses as tools for developing your marriage into one in which there is fulfillment and full expression of your individuality.

1. *Alone, without your mate present, list in one column your mate's* strengths *and in another column his or her* weaknesses. Then list your *wrong responses.* It's so easy to point a finger at your mate and so difficult to admit any personal wrongs.

After listening and evaluating what one couple's problems were, I determined that I needed to take Jane, the wife, through the steps to oneness concerning her husband, Bob. I started with the question, "What are your husband's strengths?"

"He doesn't have any."

"Lady, I know you're not too excited about what he has going for him right now. So take a minute and think. Now what are his strengths?"

"He doesn't have any!"

"There must have been something that drew you to him when you married!"

"That's why I'm here!" she said. "I can't figure out *why* I married him!"

Since I get paid for filling up columns, I pressed on to get her to list Bob's strengths; I probed and probed. Finally I hit on something when I asked, "Does he give you money each week?" She threw out a figure that was more than I was making a month. Excitedly I said, "All right, there's a strength—money!" A list is hardly one item, so I continued the search. I asked if she had her own car.

She kind of giggled and said, "Yes. Bob gave me a new El Dorado for my birthday a couple of months ago!"

"An El Dorado—that's a strength!" Well, we didn't have much, but at least we had the start of a list.

When I asked about Bob's weaknesses, her face lit up. After all, that's what she had come to discuss. The first weakness she mentioned was food. She said, "All he does is eat, eat, eat. He's 272 pounds and growing!" Then she listed the second weakness: "He doesn't pay attention to me. When he comes home in the evening he walks right to the phone. He doesn't even acknowledge that I exist!" Third, she said, "Now, he's a good man, even religious, but sometimes he gets so mad he curses me out!"

She had many more of Bob's weaknesses to share with me, but I encouraged her to move on to the next column—wrong responses. I asked, "What do you do wrong when your husband does these things?" She appeared puzzled and said, "Huh?" She seemed to have no capacity to understand that she was doing anything wrong in response to his weaknesses. Realizing that I was getting absolutely nowhere, I shifted gears and asked, "Well, what do you do when he does these horrible things?" She told me that when her husband ate too much, she had the ability to verbally assassinate the guy. At an executive party where Bob wanted to impress his boss, Jane really took a shot at him. Bob was at the chip-and-dip table across the den. Jane yelled, "Bounce over here, Bob!" I had to admit that she had a real way with words!

I asked, "What do you do when he doesn't pay attention to you?"

"I don't pay attention to him! I've got it timed now so that if he comes up to me to give me a kiss, I can turn right around and walk out of the kitchen before he even touches me." She was proud of her strategy.

"And if he curses you out?"

"I curse him right back!"

When I was going through this chart on my own mate, I discovered some interesting things. After easily filling out the strengths column, I moved to the column for weaknesses. Only one weakness kept staring me in the face: my wife seemed to be late most of the time.

If we were going to someone's home for dinner, the normal scene could be described as hectic. As the time for departure drew nigh, I stood near the front door and yelled, "Are you ready?"

When Carol appeared in the hallway, it took a quick glance to realize that if she were ready we were both in a heap of trouble! So she went back to the bedroom to continue making herself ready for the evening.

As it got later and later, my "gift" for sarcasm and cutting remarks would surface. If we were going to dinner, I'd say, "Honey, let me call and tell them we'll make it for dessert, okay?" Through this little jab I managed to arouse a reaction from her.

The verbal sparring built toward an incredibly silent yet intense atmosphere in the car. All that could be heard during the entire twenty-minute ride to the dinner was a periodic exasperated sigh! This sigh is an offensive device that warns the other person you're still steaming.

When we arrived at our destination thirty minutes late, we had to act as if nothing had happened. I opened the door for Carol and we both pasted on plastic smiles, while remaining silent. When we were greeted at the door by our host he asked, "How are you?"

"Oh, fine. Couldn't be better!" We both agreed.

2. *Admit your wrong responses to yourself and to your mate.*   I knew what Jane needed to do so I said, "You've got to admit that your responses have not been too swift. At least fifty percent of the problem is you." Actually, in her case, it was more like sixty to sixty-five percent, but I felt I should keep it even. She did finally realize that at least half of the reason for the mess she was in could be put at her own doorstep. Without this admission, it's nearly impossible to formulate any basis for healthy communication.

3. *Be thankful for your mate, especially for those areas that you don't like.* Many times, what seems to be a weakness is really just a different way of seeing a situation or a different way of doing something. By being thankful for your mate's weaknesses or differences, you can begin to see them as opportunities to complement one another toward the goal of oneness.

Carol and I recently took a test measuring our preferences in the way we value and perceive things and how we make decisions. Although after fifteen years of marriage we have certainly grown in appreciation for each other, we clarified our differences through this test even more! Again, I was reminded that many of our differences in approaching life are just that: differences, not weaknesses or competitive tactics!

4. *Look for a lesson to be learned through your mate's weaknesses.* Instead of seeing yourself in a prison of circumstances, learn to view yourself as being in a classroom of opportunity. Search for a lesson through your mate's weaknesses.

I went to my wife and asked, "Honey, what can *I* do to help *us* get ready on time?" Now, I didn't really mean that. I really meant, *What can I do to help you get over your problem of being so late?* But I said it properly: "What can *I* do to help *us* get ready on time?"

"Well, the first thing . . ." she began.

That scared me! *First* implied very strongly that there might be a *second* or even a *third* to follow. It was as if someone had prepared her for my question. She had a list!

"The first thing," she said, "is that you could hang up your clothes. You try on various combinations of clothes and let them lay all over the bedroom." I'd always wondered how my clothes made their way back on the hangers!

"Second," she continued, "you could help get the children ready for bed."

"You do that, too, huh? Okay. I'll hang up my clothes and help with the children."

"Finally," she said, "maybe you could get ready early and troubleshoot around the house when someone calls or comes to the door. Instead of yelling from the bathroom, 'Honey, would you get that?' maybe *you* could get it."

The entire dialogue sent me into a state of shock! It was as if I had walked into the bedroom with a twenty-gauge shotgun aimed directly at my wife's weaknesses—late and late—and right when I pulled the trigger, my gun blew up on *me!* What I thought was *her* problem was really *my* problem!

I realized there was a lesson to be learned from my wife's weakness, and the lesson in that particular case was not patience—although I needed a little bit of that—but becoming sensitive to the needs of my mate.

5. *Write out a commitment to your mate and read it verbally to him or her.*   Try including three items in this written commitment. First, there must be a confession without condemnation. This might be a confession of rejecting your mate in various areas or of your wrong responses. Notice I said *confession without condemnation.* Confession *with* condemnation is, "Honey, I'm so sorry I acted that way last night—but it wouldn't have happened if you. . . ." It is to be *without* condemnation! Tell the truth about yourself. Don't attempt to confess for your mate!

Second, there needs to be a resolve on your part to look beyond your mate's weaknesses and external appearances to the beauty and wholeness of the person who is there to complete you.

Third, be thankful for the one who can perfectly complete you. Receive your mate as your completor, rather than rejecting or struggling with your competitor.

These three items may not say all you want to say, but the important idea of step 5 is *verbalization.*

Bob came in to see me a few days after my session with Jane. He was so nervous! From the moment he walked in I sensed he wanted to tell me something. But each time I inquired, he stammered and stuttered and mumbled the conversation into oblivion. Finally, I was able to pin him down and help him blurt it out.

"Do you know," he said, "what my wife did yesterday? She walked over to me, kissed me, and said, 'Bob, I love you and I need you.' She really meant it!"

"What did you say?" I asked.

In an embarrassed sort of way he said, "I told her, 'I need you, too!' "

That's oneness! That's receiving your mate as your only hope for life, rather than rejecting him or her as an obstacle. Receiving your mate, focusing on his total person rather than on his weaknesses, is the only hope we all have to enjoy marital oneness and a fulfilled individuality.

Competition? No. Completion!

Part II

The Responsibility Factor: Independence or Interdependence?

3

"I. M. De Head"

In heaven all the men were separated from their wives and were asked to fall into line behind one of two signs. The sign on the left read THE HENPECKED. The sign on the right said THE HEAD. It was an incredible sight. Every husband fell into line behind THE HEN-PECKED sign—everyone, that is, except one little man. This one man, out of all husbands ever, was standing conspicuously alone behind the sign that said THE HEAD. A reporter covering the event rushed over to interview this unique man. He said, "Sir, this is unbelievable! Here you are, out of all these men, the only one standing in the line designated for husbands who have been the heads of their homes. How is it that you were able to walk into this line as the only head *ever* on earth?" The man said, "Well, I don't know. My wife just told me to stand here!"

So much of our marital humor reflects the gross misunderstanding of the idea of *headship* in the home. Because of the poverty of understanding and its disastrous effects, I guess people would rather laugh than cry about it. It is no joke! This misunderstanding of headship is hurling a crushing blow to the identity of men and women, and to the security of children, and to the very foundation of the home.

I am convinced that mates would flourish if we could begin a mass movement of restoring confidence in men to take responsibility in their homes. Men have left the responsibility of the home to their wives. Why? Because the man does not know what to do in the home or how to do it—he's confused! Consequently, some bizarre ideas of headship are prominent today.

Misconceptions of Headship

The most common misconception is to think of the head of the home as a dictator. He is not a person who gives all the orders in a dictatorial style, expecting every breath to arouse an immediate response. Some think of the head as one who must snap a bullwhip with constant demands—the master-slave relationship. This is completely wrong!

A second misconception is seeing headship as equaling perfection. I call this man "Mr. Waterwalker." He thinks his job is to have *everything* under control at all times. His goal is absolute perfection and, after all, he reasons, "when you're as together as I am, would you expect any less?" Good luck!

The third misconception is the "I.M. De Head" syndrome. This poor guy is sure that his headship needs proclamation. He's *always* ready to let everyone know that he is the head. He doesn't have a clue as to how to function as the head, so instead he gives regular speeches on the topic of his headship.

Meaning of Headship

Headship is a two-part package, according to the biblical game plan. First, it means that the man's position in the home is one of being the representative authority; second, the man's function in the home is one of being a sacrificial lover.

You may have passed out when you read the word *authority.* That word has been butchered. We see authority as automatically meaning that someone is better than someone else. That is not true! Authority is necessary so that we can move smoothly toward accomplishment. Authority is a neutral necessity to counteract chaos and to get things done.

It does not mean "better than," as is usually thought. Pure authority is much different! A good illustration of pure authority in operation is a traffic cop. When he or she blows the whistle or motions for you to stop, you stop! Why? Not because the traffic cop is better than you but because of the authority given one who wears a police badge. Pure authority does not negate equality but keeps relationships functioning more smoothly. In every relationship—home, committee, business, government—someone must ultimately be responsible or accountable in order to promote ease in decision making.

I was involved, along with three friends, in starting an organization a while back. We were so fearful of the idea of authority or that someone would be the "head" of the organization, that we decided nobody would be in charge. We were so excited and united on the idea that we didn't need a "head." The first two and one-half weeks were spent in meetings, making *big* decisions. We discussed what our stationery and business cards should look like and how many telephones we should have and big things like that. After discussing these problems at great length, we would vote, and we'd come up with 2-2 or 3-1. Then we'd team up on the holdout and threaten to firebomb his home. It was exciting! Because of our fear of authority we almost went bankrupt holding all those meetings. Authority allows for things to get done. Lack of it creates chaos!

Marital Shock Absorber

As one in authority, the husband is the shock absorber for the marriage. I look at it this way: the man is responsible for everything in the home. Now that doesn't mean that he is a better person or a dictator—it just means that the buck stops with the husband. Study after study is showing that when women take all the pressure of the home on themselves, they become less and less responsive to their husbands emotionally, psychologically, and sexually. One such study is by William Masters and Virginia Johnson and is detailed in their fine book *The Pleasure Bond*. The voice of the women's liberation movement is saying, "Listen, woman. You're being exploited. You're being used as a doormat. Get away from that clod you're with and get a better deal somewhere else." The answer, though, is not to leave for a greener pasture but to make the relationship one that works without exploitation or subjugation. Without authority, chaos reigns supreme, and the woman is the primary victim.

Marital Servant

As a sacrificial lover you are to give of yourself totally. You are responsible to be the servant of your wife-to-be, actively seeking to meet her needs. You are to give and give and give. My goal is to keep my wife off balance at all times—not tipsy, but off balance! This means I've got to constantly be thinking of ways to meet her needs. You have to become a student of your wife so that you know what makes her tick and ticked. If you never learn the difference between those two, you'll be in a heap of trouble.

You might give up a golf game or tennis match just to do something special with your wife. Maybe, just maybe, you might go shopping with her. I didn't say buy anything; just go shopping with her. Sacrificial love means doing things for and with your wife even

when it is not convenient to do them. It means focusing on the
needs of your wife, treating her like an adult and not a child, and
taking responsibility in the home. Without this dimension of sacrificial love, the man quickly becomes the dictator and woman becomes the doormat. When everything revolves around the big "I,"
marriage suffers. The man moves into the role of servant through
the function of sacrificial lover.

Ever Seen an Ugly Baby?

Sacrificial love frees you up in two ways: it frees the man from
selfishness and the woman from subjugation. I was an assistant pastor for two years. It was called *"in training."* All that means is that
I got the opportunity to do all the weird and wonderful things the
pastor didn't want to do anymore. One of my jobs was to be at the
hospital with fathers who were waiting for their wives to have
babies.

Now there is nothing uglier than someone else's baby! The kid's
head is dented and he has strange clumps of hair in stranger places.
Of course, the father would stand there and just go bananas, jumping up and down, yelling, "She looks just like me!" and "She recognizes me!" The kid didn't look like anybody, nor could she recog-
nize anyone! The father was prepared with two cameras, seven
lenses, and a movie camera, and he was using them all simultaneously. At this point I learned new ways to express my excitement
without lying about it. I found myself saying things like, "My, that
sure is a baby, isn't it?" I determined that I would never act that
way when *I* was about to become a father!

When we went to the hospital to have our first child, my wife
had to persuade me to bring the camera. I'd watched these men in
the waiting room writing letters, watching TV, or reading books.
When I began doing all three simultaneously, I knew something
strange was happening to me. And then someone called my name
and told me to move to the viewing window to see my wife and
child.

I stumbled around the corner and saw Carol, my wife, with the most beautiful baby I had ever seen. It was a girl—Tammy! She was a perfect "Gerber baby"! Right then and there I went berserk. I lost it. In the first twenty-four hours I took fifty-six slides. And the incredible thing about this absolutely beautiful baby was that she looked just like me! I'm now sure that she even recognized me! The camera just kept clicking and clicking and clicking. Then when I was permitted to hold her in my arms, I felt a love I didn't know I had in me.

By the time our second child was born I had a telephoto lens. I was a little fearful that I wouldn't be able to love another child as much as I loved Tammy. She was so special that I didn't think I had any love left for a second child. Then Tacy was born. I couldn't believe it, but the same thing happened to me all over again—I went berserk! She also was absolutely beautiful. Again I found myself wanting to give and give and give. I didn't have time to be self-centered. That's what sacrificial love is all about—it redeems us from self-centeredness.

Your sacrificial love will set your wife apart from all other women. I was so caught up in comparison and competition in relating to Carol that I never saw the need to love her sacrificially. By sacrificially loving her, I'm able to focus on her needs and find total satisfaction in her and in our relationship.

Marital Teamwork

In addition to sacrificial love, your wife needs to sense that you are on her team—to know that you are interested in and understand her frustrations and concerns.

Carol and I learned this principle firsthand when we were working at a university campus on the East Coast. I had worked for many weeks to set up a particularly important meeting with a campus official. On the day of the meeting Carol had taken Tammy (five months old) to her pediatrician.

About twenty minutes before my meeting I received word to call Carol. I called and I heard an emotional heaviness in Carol's voice.

Tammy was going to have to wear a hip brace for six months. Carol was crushed! (Now most of the time I share my numerous "clod" experiences, but this time I did the right thing.) I could have said a lot of things like, "Honey, what do you think her life expectancy is, seventy years? What's six months out of seventy years?" But instead of ridiculing her concern, I jumped on her team. "Honey, do you want me to come home?"

Her entire tone changed immediately. "No! You've got a very important meeting. I'm all right! Everything's fine!" What happened? She only needed the supportive feeling of knowing that I was on her team.

Explode Your Expectations

There's one fact that all husbands must remember: *You will never be appreciated as much as you think you ought to be appreciated.* I find that husbands have long memories of what they did right, and wives have short memories of what husbands did right. So you have this guy who is really working on overwhelming his wife, and he's taking her to Europe for vacation, or out to dinner every night for three weeks, and then she says, "You know, we don't go anywhere." This poor guy keeps bringing up his past record for her consideration, saying things like, "Did you *really* like what we did together last month?" He expects to be appreciated more than he is.

Sometimes we men get brainstorms and decide that we'll bring some flowers home. So we figure on forking over five or six dollars because, after all, it will be worth it just to see the look of ecstasy on her face.

Then you find out that flowers sold for five or six dollars about five or six years ago. You go into slight shock after shelling out twelve or fifteen dollars for some flowers, but you can just see the look of surprise on her face. This is going to be great! It's not her birthday, it's not your anniversary—just an act of pure love. An incredible move!

You pull up to the house, put the flowers behind your back, and head for the front door. After your dramatic presentation, your wife decides to dump all the day's disasters on you. She takes the flowers from you with a pleasant but weak acknowledgment, puts them on the dining-room table, and continues the dumping process. Now what are you thinking? *Look, I know Johnny broke his foot and the dog was run over and Aunt Martha is coming to stay for three weeks, but did you see the flowers?*

Just before falling asleep, you make a weak plea for just a thread of appreciation: "Did you like the flowers? They cost me almost fifteen dollars!" Husbands: just keep loving and loving and loving, because you'll never feel that you are appreciated nearly enough. Love your wife without expectation.

A Poor Investment

When my wife has a problem, I check out my contribution to it. Without fail, if my wife is in a heap of trouble, I have made a wonderful contribution to it!

While writing my first book, I allowed myself to be placed under an impossible deadline. During the last two weeks, I literally worked night and day. I worked in a small ten-by-twelve room in our apartment. Every hour or so I staggered out of the room to read my "best-seller" to Carol. Carol's job was to respond with encouraging *oohs* and *ahs* and make me another glass of iced tea.

On about the ninth or tenth day I noticed that her oohs and ahs were getting weaker, as was her tea. The way she handed me that last glass of tea communicated clearly. Her disposition said, *Hope you choke on an ice cube!* I knew I was in trouble, but I had to make my deadline! That evening, as I paused from typing to think, I heard Carol sobbing in the bedroom. I knew what the problem was. For nearly ten days I had not invested anything in our relationship. Now I was receiving a return on my investment: weak tea and tears! I went in the bedroom, sat down next to her, and said, "I know what the problem is."

Through her sobs she muttered, "You do?"

"Yes, it's me! I haven't been contributing positively to our marriage, and you're paying for it." This triggered a flood of tears that said, *I agree!*

Another poor investment made by many men is to refuse to be problem solvers. The husband must take on every problem his wife brings to him and search for solutions. It's so easy to say, "That's *your* problem! You dug the hole. Let me help you into it!" Being a problem solver means that *her* problem is *your* problem.

Surviving the Pit Hour

For a woman with young children, the most frenzied time of the day is from around four o'clock in the afternoon to when the children are in bed. This time zone has been affectionately labeled by some "the pit." I call it "the valley of the shadow"—a time when everything happens simultaneously! During this time, the children move into the kitchen because their stomachs say, "Move into the kitchen." Mom is trying to fix dinner and the kids are getting juice out (and spilling it) and making peanut-butter-and-jelly sandwiches (and dropping them). Questions are being shot at Mom every twenty-three seconds. She swats bottoms and threaten lives while animals, including those of the neighbor, move into and through the kitchen!

In the middle of the valley of the shadow, two things happen. First the phone rings. It's usually your wife's best friend, calling to see if anyone else is surviving the pit hour besides herself. Next, the doorbell rings. It's always the paperboy, who wants $3.75. Everyone senses that the big event of the day is about to take place. And sure enough, "the king" arrives home. He usually moves toward his throne, where he reads his paper and yells little tidbits of encouragement into the kitchen: "What are we having for dinner?"

"Meat loaf."

"Again?"

Then it's time for dinner and the wife has to round up the kids because they ran for their lives earlier in the evening. Finally the king takes the initiative to get everyone to the table so they can enjoy some time together. He lets loose with, "All right, get in here! Sit down! I said, sit down and shut up! All right, let's pray!" The atmosphere is not quite proper, but everyone knows that "the family that prays together stays together."

After dinner the king moves to his second throne—*the tube*. Here he watches a three-hour special about Agent 002 and observes the suave and cool way the guy operates. Pretty soon, the king is thinking to himself, *This guy is swift. This guy is cool. Hey, wait a minute. I'm swift like him. I'm cool like him.* He's getting excited about his resemblance to 002!

Meanwhile, his wife is getting the kids in and out of the bathtub, washing the dishes, cleaning up the kitchen, and putting the kids to bed. (This includes the second and third drinks of water, several potty runs, and chasing the killer boa constrictors out of the bedroom.) Then she makes one last pickup tour of the house. She staggers into the bedroom around ten o'clock and leans up against the wall. By now the king thinks he *is* Agent 002, so he says seductively, "Hey, baby, how about tonight?"

She mumbles back, "How about *what* tonight?"

In my particular situation, I realized that I had to do something with the children because I couldn't cook. We tried that once! So my job was to do something with those kids—remove them from the kitchen. For the longest time I had to come home and *wing* with my children. (That's *swing*, for those who are uninitiated.) I got so tired of "winging" that I caught myself praying for rain in the afternoon, but it sure made dinner a whole lot better.

After dinner, it's my job to clear the table and get the dishes over to the dishwasher while Carol puts the children in the tub. Then while Carol fills the dishwasher and cleans up the kitchen, I'm getting the kids out of the tub and dressed for bed. When I function as head during the valley of the shadow, we're able to cut the time required by over an hour. Now we can stagger into the bedroom *together* and enjoy each other.

There is no headship unless you function in "the valley of the shadow." Will you commit yourself to being the shock absorber and servant in your home?

4

So Who Wants to Be a Doormat?

Doormats serve one purpose only—to wipe the dirt off of your shoes. *So who wants to be a doormat?*

There is a whole lot of misunderstanding over the woman's role in the home, and especially over one loaded word: *submission*. The women's movement has sought to show that women are basically subjugated and exploited. The woman is the doormat of the world! For the most part I agree with this evaluation of the problems

women face in our world. Because of the confusion over what it means for a woman to be a helpmate to her husband, and the consequent foolish teaching on the topic, the current blurriness in what femaleness actually means has resulted. However, I don't agree with any solutions which suggest running away from home in order for women to find respect and a feeling of self-identity. Self-identity is not found in a vacuum but in relationships.

Another emotional reaction has arisen from many well-meaning women who defend the doormat life-style. This is a very popular approach within many religious circles. There are at least two lines of thought. One proposes that women are inferior to men; women must accept this fact and make the best out of it. The other encourages women to be aggressive within their doormat life-style. The goal is to be giddy women playing silly games in relating to their husbands. In many instances, this is nothing more than a fantasy trip into immaturity.

Misconceptions of a Helpmate

Much of what is portrayed as qualities of a woman who is a helpmate to her husband is absolute foolishness. No wonder it's not a popular profile! There are three pervasive misconceptions regarding a helpmate.

Slave Girl

This is the woman who has your basic ball-and-chain view of what being a helpmate is all about. She is locked in her house, only relating to the outside world through soap operas and supermarkets. She is a terrible bore to be around, and exists solely to serve "the king." She rarely, if ever, gets appreciation for all the work she accomplishes for his highness.

Speechless

In this case, the woman is forbidden to say a word—especially one which contradicts that of the king. She is not to speak unless spoken to, and is constantly awaiting the master's next breath to direct her.

Brain on Shelf

Notice that her brain is equal to mustard and pickles. This woman is not permitted to think at all. Even if she were allowed, she would probably be unable to do so. A fashion magazine provides her with all the intellectual stimulation she needs for a month.

Meaning of Helpmate

In defining *helpmate*, there are two things that it is *not*. First, it is not a status of inferiority. The purpose of submission is to allow two people to function as a team in order to complement each other instead of competing with each other.

Second, being a helpmate is not primarily an action but an attitude. There are times when my wife is with me geographically, but her attitude leaves a little to be desired. A woman may claim that she is a wonderful helpmate because she has actually complied with her husband's wishes. However, if you were to ask the husband, he would say that his wife's attitude made her actions meaningless. The difference in perspective lies in the fact that she was thinking in terms of action, but her attitude was showing. And that's what he saw! The *way* something is done makes all the difference in the world.

A woman needs to always be aware of the two dimensions of her husband's headship: that of representative authority (shock absorber) and that of sacrificial lover (servant). She needs to pick up on these two dimensions whenever she sees her man exercising them, and encourage him like crazy. How do you do that? Well, when you see your husband exercising responsible authority in the home, respond to that authority. Get on his team. Support him! Your response will move your relationship toward oneness as your husband feels the respect you have for him. This response to him is *not* because he is better than you but because you want to assure him that he can count on your being on his team. When your husband exercises responsible authority, support him!

When your husband moves in to act as a sacrificial lover, encourage him. The great majority of men want to give love but they just don't know how. Some men figure that giving money is the same as giving love. The more expensive the gift, they reason, the more love they have shown. As a wife, you need to encourage your man when you sense that he is trying to show you love. Get excited when he buys a garbage disposal for you! He is trying to show his love for you. Men excel at showing love in material ways. Show him how to love you by appreciating his expression of love and letting him know what you want.

Model of a Helpmate

Wives need to move in the direction of voluntary submission to their husbands for the sake of oneness in their marriages. What does voluntary submission mean? Does it mean that you are to keep your mouth shut at all times and obey the king? In order to get a clearer picture, let's talk about voluntary submission for the sake of oneness.

Resistance Syndrome

Oneness is destroyed by the *resistance syndrome*. A constant, gnawing resistance against your husband will push him into a corner, forcing him to either snap back at you or retreat altogether. The Book of Proverbs has the best statement of this principle that I have seen. Proverbs says that a woman who keeps offering resistance after a decision has been made is like rain on a tin roof—she just keeps dripping and dripping and dripping.

A man offers to take his family out to dinner on the spur of the moment. As he begins driving away, he'll usually say, "Honey, where would you like to eat?"

"Oh, I don't care. You decide!" After a few seconds of thought he suggests, "Let's go for hamburgers." His wife responds, "Hamburgers? You really want to go for hamburgers?"

"You don't want to go for hamburgers, I take it?"

"Oh, it doesn't make any difference to me. You make the decision," she says.

"Okay. Then let's go for burgers."

"Hamburgers, huh? We had them two weeks ago. You really want them again? *Well, it's your decision!*" she says. Dripping and dripping and dripping!

Sometimes husbands get brilliant ideas. Maybe you are on your way to a friend's house after dinner and your husband is going to surprise you by swinging by the ice-cream shop before you arrive at their house. So you're driving along and all of a sudden he makes a right turn instead of a left turn. What happens? You say, "Where are you going? I can't believe it! We've gone to this house at least a hundred times before, and now you make a wrong turn! You're going in the opposite direction. I can't believe it!"

You know what he's thinking now? *I may get an ice-cream cone . . . but she won't!* Dripping and dripping and dripping! Your resistance just keeps wearing away the relationship. Resistance is not the same as expressing an opinion or disagreement. You can disagree without being disagreeable!

Woman: The Glory of the Man

Along with offering no resistance after a decision is made, the wife who wants to be a helpmate is to reflect her husband positively. Earlier we said that the husband is to set his wife apart as being special among all other women. What this means is that the woman needs to respond to her husband and seek to be the type of woman he desires to set apart. The cycle might look like this:

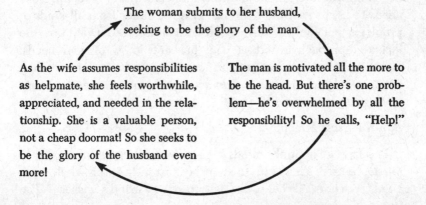

The woman submits to her husband, seeking to be the glory of the man.

As the wife assumes responsibilities as helpmate, she feels worthwhile, appreciated, and needed in the relationship. She is a valuable person, not a cheap doormat! So she seeks to be the glory of the husband even more!

The man is motivated all the more to be the head. But there's one problem—he's overwhelmed by all the responsibility! So he calls, "Help!"

A positive reflection of your husband is being the glory of the man. Many times I'll hear women say, "Well, you know my husband. You know George, and I can tell you right now that he isn't going to buy this or do that." That is not reflecting positively—that's running him down. How do you reflect your husband? It's a winning combination when the wife is reflecting her husband positively and he is loving her sacrificially.

I know what you're thinking. *What if it's only a one-way relationship? What if I'm doing my part, but my mate doesn't budge?* There are many ways of approaching a "one-way marriage," some of which we will discuss in this chapter. But let's not get bogged down by your mate. *You are responsible for your actions,* so let's continue sharpening the focus on *your* responsibility!

You cannot reflect your husband positively and motivate him to meet your needs if he doesn't know what your needs are. So much of marriage is spent in a cat-and-mouse game. Many times it's the wife who's thinking, *I've got a need, but you don't know what it is! If you can figure out what it is, it's going to be super around the ranch. But if you can't figure it out, it's going to be pretty rough around here for weeks!* So the husband finally figures out what her need is and then begins to make an attempt to meet it. At this point the wife lets him know, verbally or nonverbally, that it's too late! Most men are not too swift at picking up a woman's subtle, nonverbal clues. We need to be told, point-blank sometimes, what you need and what we can do to meet that need. By not revealing your needs to us, you set the relationship up to suffer from all kinds of problems that could be easily dealt with if discussed. Don't take the lockjaw approach in letting your husband know of your needs. *Submission is more than support, encouragement, and responding to your husband. There is also an active element of submitting your feelings and thoughts.*

Ban the Bible Study?

Red flags go up in the minds of most women when the word *submission* is used. They want to know how far to take this whole idea. In other words, "When can I ignore my husband's wishes?" The principle is this: *A wife finds fulfillment in life as she submits to her husband, up to the point of violating her personal conscience.*

At one Bible-study group I met a very strange woman. She walked up after the study and said, "I'm sure you'll agree with me when I say that God wants me here at this Thursday-morning Bible study."

"Well, I'm sure that God is happy with your presence here."

She continued, "Even though my husband doesn't like my coming here, God wants me here, right?"

"Oh, well," I said, "that makes it a completely different story."

She went on. "You and I both know that the Bible says I should be at this Thursday-morning meeting."

I realized I had a real winner on my hands. I asked if she could find those passages in the Bible that convinced her she should be at this study group. She eagerly complied with my request. She sat over in the corner of the dining room and began flipping madly through her Bible. After most of the women had gone, she approached me with a somber look on her face.

"You're a minister, aren't you?"

"Well, kind of," I answered.

"Have you read the Bible through a few times?" she asked.

I said, "Yes, a few times."

"Well," she said, "have you ever read the passages I'm talking about?"

"No, I can't say I have," I replied.

"That's what I thought," she said sadly. "What do you think I should do?"

I said, "Well, to tell you the truth, for the sake of oneness in your marriage, I think you ought to go home and not come back here on Thursdays."

"What would God think?" she asked.

"I think God would be impressed," I answered.

Ban the Church?

Sometimes women come to me complaining about their tyrant husbands who will not let them go to church. They're sure that this is a situation in which they should be able to tell them to take a hike. In each case of this type that I've counseled, the wife had set up a preaching ministry in the home. She had set up her pulpit and had religious books piled three feet deep all over the living room. So the husband started thinking, *If I can shut off the source of her supply, I won't get this garbage anymore.* In each case I suggested that the wife shut down her preaching activities in the house and stop attending church for three or four Sundays. Then she was to ask her husband if she could go to church. In every case (because his real reason for putting a stop to church attendance was removed) the husband allowed his wife to return to church. In fact, a couple of them acted surprised that their wives hadn't been going, and actually encouraged them to go!

How About Swapping Mates?

What happens if your husband wants to engage in a little wife swapping? Again, you must look at the real reason behind your husband's request, instead of exploding with emotion. Could it be that he wants something more sexually than what he is experiencing with you? He is probably bored with you and you need to deal with that instead of throwing it back in his face with comments such as, "You're no Tom Selleck yourself, you know!" After discerning the real reason behind the request, suggest creative ways of meeting his basic need without violating your personal conscience. In this specific instance, you must overwhelm your husband sexually—meet his needs creatively. If you do this, you can bet he won't be interested in swapping you with *anybody!*

There may be times when your husband asks you to do something that violates your personal conscience. You try to meet the real need behind his request by suggesting or implementing a creative alternative, but he still wants you to do this thing. This is the time you have to say, "I'm sorry, honey, but I won't do that." *Submission for the sake of oneness in the marriage, up to the point of violating your personal conscience.* It's part of a game plan that works!

Creativity and Surprise

Successful wives have one thing in common: they are all students of their husbands. What are his needs? What does he really enjoy? This will take some creativity and surprise. Early in our marriage, Carol began a practice that has been a real lift to me. When I come home from the office, she and our girls are all dressed up nicely to greet me. (This isn't the king-arriving-home routine. We don't have the slipper-and-newspaper bit at our house during "the valley of the shadow.") No matter how worn out I am from the day's pressures, this greeting is refreshing!

Just think, for a moment, what many husbands go through in a typical day in relation to their wives. The husband leaves home for work; his wife sends him on his way. He carries a vision of his wife to work. Her roller-and-pin-curl system gives the appearance of being wired for sound. She's wearing a ten-year-old robe, full of rips and snags, with only two buttons surviving. She has a new one in the closet, but refuses to give up the sentimental standby. As the husband arrives at his job, he notices that there isn't another woman in the building who looks like his wife did this morning— not one! Now, actually the morning scene isn't so bad, because that is an accepted part of life. The real problem occurs when the husband arrives home and his wife looks a little more tattered than she did early that morning!

Another thing my wife does that I enjoy is that she secretly sends love notes in my suitcase when I travel to a conference. She uses the element of surprise as she writes these juicy little notes and hides them in my suitcase. She doesn't always do this. If she sent a note on every trip, it would begin to lose its effect.

Too Practical for Pleasure

In addition to suggesting the use of creativity and surprise in loving and pleasing your husbands, I want to insert a caution: be careful of being too practical. Women have a tendency to operate under the philosophy that anything less than pure practicality is wasteful. There are some things which seem wasteful yet can be an important ingredient in solidifying your marital relationship. This more than compensates for any "waste." It's an investment in your marital oneness!

For instance, women can be too practical on vacations. After driving for twelve hours, I head for the first sign that says MOTEL. All I want is a bed with no bugs in it. That's it! But Carol wants us to shop around at five or six other motels to see where we can get the best deal. I could fall asleep looking for a bed! Too practical!

Several years ago I had been speaking at marriage seminars for several weekends (ten) in a row. That was during a time in my life that I wasn't winning any awards for brilliance in personal scheduling. Anyway, after the last weekend was over, I boarded a plane for home and began to plan a getaway for our family, effective immediately upon my arrival at home. When I got there I said, "Honey, how long will it take you to get the family packed and in the car?"

She looked me directly in the eyes and confidently said, "One hour!"

"Well," I said, "whoever and whatever is out in the 'blue bomb' in one hour is going on a trip with me."

And we did go away and had a fantastic time! That was one time I did not need to hear seventeen reasons this trip was impractical and ridiculous. I was grateful to Carol that she wasn't dripping!

I take my wife out to dinner or lunch once a week whether she needs it or not! That may not be practical, but I see it as an investment in our relationship. Be a student of your husband and allow him to do some impractical things that he feels will enhance your oneness.

An Expensive Woman!

The Bible calls a woman who is beautiful on the inside *precious*, which means rare or expensive! This inner beauty is descriptive of a woman who is focused on her responsibility of pleasing her husband. She has a gentle and quiet spirit and delights in cultivating oneness with her man.

Are you becoming a rare and expensive woman in your husband's sight? Are you dying to yourself by voluntarily submitting to your husband's authority in your home for the sake of oneness in your marriage? You submit to him not because he is better or smarter but because you'll lose if you demand your rights. You'll lose the very thing you are demanding every time, and you'll lose something else—your marriage!

The responsibility factor helps to put marriage into focus: one head and one helpmate working together toward oneness and never asking who is the greater of the two. That's a maximum marriage. And that is the only type of marriage that works!

In the middle of the morning, Mrs. Harvey noticed a donkey in her front yard. She immediately called the people from the animal control center. But after they arrived, she had a bright idea! She asked the two men, "If I were to give each of you twenty dollars, would you put this donkey in my upstairs bathtub?" The men refused! Then she increased the fee to fifty dollars each. The men agreed, struggled to put the donkey in the bathtub, and then asked in wonderment, "Why in this world would you pay so much money to put a donkey in your bathtub?"

Mrs. Harvey answered, "For over thirty years my husband has come home from work each night and asked the same question: 'What's new today?' So tonight I'm going to tell him!"

Whatever else you do, tell your husband what's new!

5

Women Are Weird and Men Are Strange[1]

In 1970, 96 percent of all Americans declared themselves dedicated to the ideal of two people sharing a life and a home together. A decade later the number was precisely the same—a virtually universal 96 percent! Why, then, do we experience the battle of the sexes at every level of society?

I'm convinced that the battle lingers on because we continually violate the most basic principle of the sexes: difference! We strive for equality (which is desirable) and achieve sameness (which is destructive)! But men and women are incurably different. And it's only when we understand that difference that we are free to be complementary to one another.

When not demonstrating for equality, we carefully put our masks in place and play the *roles* that have gradually become comfortable! Roles may be comfortable, but they are not for real. When people play their roles they don't relate. On the contrary, playing roles turns a relationship into empty ritual and cold routine! Disappointed by this hollow shell of a relationship, people desperately search for another one. They hope *this* one will work. In most cases, this *new* venture slips into the need for *new* roles, with new masks, to play a different game! But 96 percent of us keep trying to make it work!

The only possible way to end this great sexual war is to sharpen the focus on the complementary difference between men and women. I'm a firm believer that women are weird and men are very strange!

Do You Love Me?

A women will ask her man, "Do you love me?" (It's 8:00). "Are you sure?" (8:10). "You really do?" (8:15). "You do, huh?" (8:20). In the meantime, her man is thinking (and perhaps saying), "I told you I loved you when we were married. And it's still in effect until I revoke it!" Now that's a big difference!

That same kind of difference is illustrated when a couple receives an invitation to a party. The woman's response is, "What shall I wear?" and the man's, "How can I get out of this?"

In the Now or Out There Somewhere?

Most woman initially respond in the immediate—*in the now!* They are rarely "out there," but live right here in the now. Most men initially respond in long-range manner. They are rarely here, but live out there somewhere!

Years ago I came home enthusiastically announcing that we were going to the Middle East for a short tour! Carol's response was like a cold, wet blanket on my excitement. I was looking forward to this trip eight months in the future, and she asked me four questions in the *now!* They were: How can we afford it? Who will keep the kids? What will we do with the house? What about the car? All my enthusiasm was quickly dampened!

But it wasn't her fault! She was simply acting characteristically as woman. I should have realized that she was viewing this situation in the now. My mistake was to ignore the *now!* I could have approached it in this way: "Honey, I have a topic sentence and a few things to follow. Topic sentence: We're going to the Middle East! *Hold it!* It's paid for. I know who will keep the kids. I believe we'll leave the house right here, and we'll put the car in the garage!" I would have met her need of the immediate and freed her up to get excited in the long-range future!

The flip side of this frustration happens when the man comes home from work. You see, most women make a false assumption when they see their husbands' bodies coming through the door. *The woman assumes that her husband came home with his body!* But he did not! He sent his body on ahead to meet the deadline so he wouldn't be badgered all night. He's not there. He's *out there* somewhere expanding and developing his business or looking for a deal, but he's not here, in the now!

If your man is out there somewhere, you must tell him that he is home now. I think Marabel Morgan's suggestion in *The Total Woman* is a bit excessive. She suggests that you greet your man at the door wearing boots and, well, just boots! I believe most men, when greeted in this manner, would say, "Oh, excuse me!" thinking they had the wrong house! Tell your husband he's home. Talk about how good it is to be at home with him. Then feed him something. This may be the only clue man is able to discern—food! Once you have fed him, you are likely to notice an incredible change in him—a change from out there somewhere to living in the now!

Possess or Be Possessed?

Man has an inner female and woman has an inner male. If a man possesses his inner female, he exudes warmth, sensitivity, and healing. But when he is possessed by his inner female, he goes into a strange moodiness. He goes into a passive, withdrawn state, vaguely blaming others for his mood. In this state, he is unavailable for relating to people—especially his wife!

When a woman experiences the dark side of her man's inner female, she tries to bail him out of this horrible mood. But this is the absolute worst thing she could do in the midst of his female attack! She now gets rebuffed by her husband, because he is unable to relate to her in this state. This triggers the dark side of her inner male, and she has a male attack! She is filled with criticism, judgment, and angry opinions against him! Now there are two people who are possessed by their inner counterparts and in no way capable of relationship! Both man and woman must learn to control their inner capacities for relationship. *Possess yourself or be possessed by yourself!*

When your man is having a female attack, let him have his attack all by himself. There is nothing you can do to help! In the same way, when your woman is having a male attack, do not react against her! Her anger will surely bruise you!

Thinkers and Feelers

Understanding maleness and femaleness is a great aid in knowing how to communicate to your mate or other family member. *Most males think first and then feel. Most females feel first and then think.* In light of this, a woman must never ask her man how he feels until she pulls out of him what he thinks. So the first question asked of a man must be, "What do you think?"

Conversely, a man must never, ever ask a woman what she thinks until after he inquires about how she feels. She will tell you what she thinks, but she will initially communicate her thoughts through her feelings. When this is not followed, women suspect that their husbands have no feelings and men believe their wives are unable to think.

Both are completely mistaken, because their initial, and possibly total, approach to the opposite sex is all wrong. A simple biblical principle corrects the perspective. It says, "Let each individual among you also love his own wife even as himself; and let the wife see to it that she respect her husband" (Ephesians 5:33).

According to this and various psychological studies, a man primarily needs respect and a woman primarily needs love and cherishing. It becomes a vicious cycle! If a woman isn't cherished by her man, she will not respect him. And if a man doesn't get respect, it is very difficult for him to cherish his wife.

A man needs respect, but he can easily become bankrupt in this area through two extreme behaviors. The first extreme is to be demanding about it. You can't demand respect—especially by being verbally or physically abusive! Another extreme is to be walking on eggs—playing the part of a Milquetoast. She can only respect a man who is a man—responsible and caring.

A woman needs to be cherished. And when she isn't, she becomes increasingly hard and brittle—almost unlovable. She must be careful not to become a "clinging vine," begging her man to cherish, or a "Bloody Mary" who becomes caustic in nagging him toward cherishing. A man can only cherish a woman who is a woman—respectful and supportive.

Marital Nuclear Bomb!

As a man, I've learned exactly what it means to cherish a woman. My wife came into the living room announcing to me that a "nuclear bomb" had just exploded in the back bedroom. In all my wisdom, knowledge, and vast counseling experience, I immediately moved into gear and gave her the answer to her problem in the back bedroom. But now she turned on me! She didn't want an answer to her problem. All she wanted to know was, "Do you *care?*

Do you *care* that a nuclear blast just happened in the back bedroom? Because if you *care*, I'll go back and clean it up! But if you don't *care*, there will be another nuclear blast right here in the living room!" A woman needs to know that her man cares—that he cherishes her!

Have you seen the license plate frame which says, TO KNOW ME IS TO LOVE ME? This is precisely what the concept of weird women and strange men is all about. The more understanding you have of each other, the better able you are to express your love. The very essence of love is constantly saying, "Please understand me!" *When I feel understood, I feel loved!*

From Ritual to Relationship

Man plus woman need not become a ritual. Stress in the family will be greatly reduced when man and woman stop role playing and start relating. *Men—control your inner female and cherish your wife! Women—control your inner male and respect your husband!*

A four-year-old girl and a three-year-old boy who were playing house walked up to a neighbor's house and rang the doorbell. When the neighbor lady opened the door, the little girl said, "Hello! We are playing house. This is my husband and I am his wife! May we come in?" The lady went along with their role playing and said, "Oh, do come in!" She then seated them in the family room and served them lemonade and cookies. They talked for a few minutes and then the kind lady offered her visitors another glass of lemonade. The little girl answered the offer, "No, thank you! We have to go now. My husband just wet his pants!" That's just the kind of thing that can happen while masquerading in your roles rather than melting into a real relationship! *Stop role playing and start relating!*

6

First Things First

Priorities are for people. Someone once said that we are always complaining that our days are few, and acting as though there would be no end to them! You will never *find* time for anything. If you want time you must *make* it. We are all given the same twenty-four-hour day, but it is for us to decide how we will spend that time.

Priorities are referring to the quality of time more than the quantity. A priority item is an important one that must precede something else. Most people are too busy or are under extreme pressure to get things done. With few exceptions, each one is wrestling with what to do next rather than with what is to be done ultimately.

We need priorities in order to make decisions that will produce peace instead of pressure. Some of the most intense pressures in life are created by the inability to say no. The result? Either a person is intimidated into saying yes to something that warranted a no, or he is burdened down with guilt after blurting out an unsettled no. Either way is pressurized. There is the pressure of doing too much, or the guilt of saying no!

Proper priorities will free you from unnecessary pressures. I used to feel guilty for taking a day off or turning down a speaking opportunity. But not anymore! I have a new freedom to say no, based on my priorities.

One word of caution before we go through these key priorities. You may feel that you have only to conquer this problem of priorities once and for all. The truth is that you will have to fight like crazy to maintain your priorities. Believe me, it is a daily fight! Sometimes you may cruise along, well in control because you have been living and making decisions on the basis of your priorities. Frequently, though, you will find yourself controlled by circumstances and the pressure of other people who are convinced that they have a wonderful plan for your life. That's the time you must go back to your priorities.

Your Key Priorities

The *first priority* is to develop a God consciousness, coming into a relationship with the Designer of the family so that you can experi-

ence the design. This is the supernatural factor, and it is a nonnegotiable one if you want to experience the game plan for family living.

The *second priority* is your relationship with your mate. Many men find it easy to slip their vocation into this slot, while women will frequently put their children or home in this place.

I've talked with many men over the years who complain that their wives are extremely negative and naggingly resistant when they want to go out with the guys to hunt, golf, or play tennis. In such cases the wife is not down on hunting or golfing or tennis but is screaming for attention to the priorities of the marriage. In each situation, I've counseled the man to evaluate and rework his priorities, emphasizing his need to cultivate an intimate, personal relationship with his wife. After laying this foundation of a relationship, the wife loses her need to be resistant and negative. In some cases she may even be excited about his activities.

The *third priority* is your children. I'm convinced that parents could fail miserably in the area of discipline, being either too permissive or too authoritarian, and still succeed if there is a healthy relationship. Although priorities are referring to quality of time more than quantity of time, be careful not to use that as a cop-out. Relationships take time. You'll never regret taking time each week to relate individually to your children.

Many times the husband or wife or both will verbalize a need to get away for a couple of days. Then, of course, *the* question comes up: "What will we do with the kids?" The kids will enjoy the time away from you, believe me, and will probably say, "Hey, could you go away again next week?" You will be better parents because of the renewed closeness resulting from your time together. The child's primary base of security comes from your relationship to your mate, so take time to get away by yourselves.

Your vocation is your *fourth priority.* Perhaps you are both working or maybe the wife is a homemaker, which means she is working more than her husband!

The *fifth priority* is your social relationships—those that are outside the home or vocation.

These five priorities—God consciousness, your mate, your children, your vocation, and your social relationships—should determine where you spend your quality time. It becomes very easy to emphasize those priorities which are at the end of the list and to neglect the top priorities. Problems result when we don't know how to say no.

A man came into my office for counseling and said, "My business is number one and my wife is number two."

"Well," I said, "that's really exciting. Do you realize that is probably why you are here?"

This guy was really proud of his priorities. He had worked them all out himself, and that's why he was sitting in my office. He couldn't continue doing what he needed to do at work without having his wife on his team. When I speak at corporation seminars I always point out that the best production comes from those executives and employees who are winning at home. Only when a person's priorities are straight can he or she feel free enough to move out and be the person he should be in his vocation. It's when you don't take time for your priority relationships that you are asking for trouble.

Learning to Say No

When I first graduated from seminary, I was speaking anywhere anybody asked me. At the end of a couple of years I realized that I would be dead very shortly if that kind of pace were kept up. So I began to take Mondays off. I was so excited about taking that day off that I would write it in my calendar, underline it in red ink, and put exclamation points by it. Then it would happen—the phone would ring. There would end my day off. Someone on the other end of the phone would explain the wonderful plan he had for my day and how this or that *had* to be done. Sometimes opening mail would ruin the day. On Mondays I often contemplated assassinating the mailman. I got to the point where I refused to check into the rat race on Mondays. I learned to say no!

The moment I held to my convictions concerning my priorities, I began to sense that Carol was becoming more and more excited about being on my team. Now I take Mondays off—no phone calls, no mail reading, no counseling. If somebody threatens to shoot himself on Monday I ask if he can postpone it until Tuesday. It's the only way I can stay alive.

A minister once called me and said, "God has told me [and when people start out like that it really bugs me] that you are to be our speaker on marriage and the family this spring."

"That's really exciting," I said, "but I hope He told you the date, because I don't have any open days."

He said, "Yes, I found out yesterday when I called your office. I did a little investigating and found out that you have an open date."

"Really, when is it?" I asked.

"Easter," he said.

"That's not open," I replied.

He was puzzled. "You're speaking someplace?"

I said, "No."

"Ah," he said, "then it's still open!"

"No, it's been closed for a long time, actually," I said.

"Well, what are you doing?" he asked.

"My family and I are going up to a cabin in the mountains," I said.

"On Easter?" he wondered.

"Oh, yeah," I said. "The cabin is there all year round, you know."

Then came the weird part. "Are you still in the ministry?" he asked.

I said, "Yes, but not on Easter."

He questioned me further. "Will you be going to church up there?"

"Well," I said, "I hadn't thought about it. I'm not sure there's a church up there. I suppose if there is one, we might sneak in the back, I don't know."

"And you are still in the ministry?" he asked again.

"Yes, but not on Easter," I replied.

The most exciting word in my vocabulary is *no!* It frees me to enjoy my priority relationships.

The Most Important Priority

Let's take a look at the first priority—developing a God consciousness. Why is the supernatural factor necessary? We've talked about Plan B and why it works, so why bring in the supernatural? Why do we have to bring God into this whole deal?

I see two reasons that we all need the supernatural factor to make Plan B work: first to *absolve the guilt;* second to *apply the glue.*

We need the supernatural factor to absolve the guilt. A man came to my office one day and started chatting. After a short while he asked, "What really makes a good marriage?"

I said, "That's a good question. There's the oneness factor, the responsibility factor, the intimacy factor, and the supernatural factor." When I got to the supernatural factor he jumped up and asked, "What's that?"

"Well," I said, "it takes a miracle to pull off any marriage these days."

"I'll buy that," he replied.

The next week we met again and went through the oneness factor. After that came the responsibility factor. I really had to work through that one with this guy. At one point I said, "Listen. You haven't a flicker of either of those. I mean, you haven't even stumbled into them by accident. Most people will at least stumble in, but not you. You haven't been in the ball park at all with this woman of yours."

"Well," he said, "where's the miracle? Isn't it time to go over that miracle thing yet?"

"Yeah, we'll hit it next week," I replied.

The next week I began to move into the intimacy factor with him and he just cut me off. "Would you get to the miracle thing? That's what I need. I don't think anything else will work."

"Good point," I said. "What is your biggest problem right now?"

"Well, I'm guilty," he said.

"Why are you guilty?" I asked.

"I just feel guilty," he replied.

"Why?" I asked again.

He said, "Because I am guilty, that's why."

"That's good," I said. "In fact, that's very good, because many people don't realize that they are guilty. I have four things you can do for your guilt."

"Oh, good. I wanted to find out some way of getting rid of my guilt," he said.

"The first three don't work," I said.

He got mad. "Then why are you going to tell them to me?"

"I just want to tell them to you because I think it's important that you have the first three," I said. "They don't work, but the fourth works."

He was a little put out, but said, "Okay, give them to me."

"The first one," I said, "is to transfer the guilt. Just act as if it's your mate's fault. No doubt about it, she has been a real witch during this whole thing. If you can't blame your mate, lay it all on your upbringing. After all, you have enough terrible childhood memories to cover your behavior for years. Or, how about society? Society is sick, sick, sick, and it never helped you out when you needed it. Just transfer all your guilt to someone or something. You've got five or six people, easily, whom we can blame this whole mess on."

He said, "I tried that. It worked well for a while, but it didn't last."

"Second," I said, "maybe we could lower the standard. We could act as though you didn't break a standard after all. Why should you feel guilty?"

"Yeah, why should I feel guilty?" he echoed.

"Do you still feel guilty?" I asked.

"Yeah," he replied.

"Well," I said, "just lower the standard. So you've hurt your wife and kids and messed your business up? Just lower your standards. The key is to keep repeating, 'I'm not doing anything different from what millions of others are doing.' The disintegration of a standard usually goes like this: in the first step you say, 'Well, it all depends on how you look at it'; in the second step, you say, 'It doesn't make any difference how you look at it'; and in the final step you just start saying, 'I don't think anybody knows how to look at it!' Through this process you can disintegrate any moral standard you want. So just lower your standards."

"I can't live with that. It doesn't work," he said.

"Okay. Now the third option has potential, but I can't ever get anyone to try it," I said.

He asked, "What is it?"

"Well," I said, "you could move."

"What do you mean?" he asked.

I continued. "You could move far away so that no guilt can be put on you, because nobody will know you."

"I tried that," he said. "I moved to Seattle for three days and just sat there in a motel. I just died in a pile up there. I didn't see anyone and I still felt guilty. Where would you suggest that I move?"

"Every time I've ever suggested it, I've suggested a move to Tierra del Fuego," I said.

"Why is that?" he asked.

"Do you know anybody there?"

"No," he said.

"That's the point. But," I continued, "none of these three ways works. The fourth one is what works, and that is where you let God take care of the guilt." I then explained the supernatural factor to him.

The Supernatural Factor

I'm not a fan of religion at all. Religion died a long time ago—it's just that no one has gotten around to burying it yet. I grew up in a strict religious system. I was told that if I wanted to get my ticket, I would have to refrain from doing fifteen things. Of course I asked to look at the list of *don'ts* so that I could check the fine print. I wanted to know how much this ticket was going to cost me.

Well, after checking out that list of fifteen *don'ts*, I realized I was in big trouble because that list represented my goals in life. So I asked if I could see the list of things I could do. As I looked over those five things, I went into shock—they were all meetings. The list included church on Sunday morning, Sunday evening, and Wednesday evening, along with a Bible study on Thursday morning and a meeting on Saturday night just to make sure that I didn't enjoy the weekend. Right there I decided that the price of a ticket was a little steep.

I went to another group and said I wanted a ticket, plain and simple. I told them I didn't want any frills or fancy meals on the flight—just the ticket. This group got excited and told me, "We'll give you a ticket! Just come along with us and let us dunk you in our tank, or squirt you or sprinkle you or dry-clean you or drown you." I didn't think that it sounded so bad, so I tried it. You know what happened? I got a wet body, that's all!

I don't like religion because it is a system of do's and don'ts that doesn't work. A lot of people dismiss the Bible as garbage because they see it as part of a religious system. But the Bible gives a plan as to how a person can have a relationship with God, and through that relationship absolve his guilt. Everyone is trying to get rid of guilt. Some people get rid of guilt by hating themselves, or getting depressed, or even committing suicide. Everybody feels as though they have to pay for their guilt.

When Jesus arrived on the scene, He didn't set up a religious system. In fact, He was down on religion. I mean, *really down.* The religious leaders of the day asked Him what He thought of them and He said, "Two words come to mind. One is *snakes.* Want the other? Try *painted tombstones.*" Now there aren't too many positive ways of looking at those two words! Jesus did not come to set up an ethical religious system. Jesus came for one purpose—to make a payment. Throughout all of biblical history, through the sacrifices and various methods of dealing with human guilt, there is a looking forward to a Person who would come to make the ultimate and final payment for guilt.

Look at it this way. Let's say you wrote down every sin you ever committed. Some people think that sin means either rape, murder, or adultery, and since they haven't done any of those lately, they are home free. But the Bible says that sin is an attitude that works itself out in actions. It's an attitude that says, "Listen, God. Why don't You go Your way and I'll go mine. I'll check in with You when I'm seventy-five and we'll see if we can't negotiate something." If we were to write down each sin we had committed, some of us would have longer lists than others. Some would be producing ten-volume sets of lists. I, of course, could list mine on one side of a three-by-five-inch card. The point is that it doesn't matter how long your list is—it must be paid for by death. We have two choices, according to the Bible. We can pay for it ourselves for eternity or we can accept God's plan of paying for our sins through the death of Jesus. Jesus is God's only authorized substitutionary payment plan. That, pure and simple, is the Bible's solution to our guilt problem.

You may wonder how one man can pay for all of your guilt before God. It's because of Jesus' claim to be God in human flesh, and His support of that claim through His life, teachings, and Resurrection that He is able to erase your list and its accompanying guilt.

At one point in the Bible Jesus comes right out and says, "If you've seen Me you've seen God" (see John 14:9). The religious leaders became irritated with Him and asked, "Hey, tell us. Are You the One whom the Old Testament calls the Messiah?" Jesus said, "You got it. That's Me."

C. S. Lewis, the great Cambridge scholar, said that we really have only three options as far as what to believe about Jesus. First, He could have been a flat-out liar. If He lied, then He was awfully dumb because He eventually died for what He knew was baloney. Plus, He preached against lying and hypocrisy, and it would be totally inconsistent with His whole life to be lying about His basic identity. The second option is that Jesus was just plain nuts. Maybe He was prone toward hallucinations and visions of grandeur. Lewis pointed out that one doesn't show the kind of character, compassion, and wisdom that Jesus showed if he is a nut. The Bible indicates that Jesus came with many convincing proofs, among them His Resurrection from the dead, to show that He is the God-man who has the power and authority to deal with our guilt.

The supernatural factor not only deals with absolving our guilt but it also helps in applying the glue. Happy marriages are made by healthy people—those who know who they are and how to deal with their guilt, and who have a relationship with their Designer. *Redbook Magazine* recently came out with some statistics showing that those who indicated they had a relationship with God also indicated that they enjoyed life more and enjoyed sex more! The supernatural factor makes a difference in the home—it's the glue that gives cohesion and purpose to your family and to your identity.

Plan B won't happen by accident but only as you cultivate your priority relationships in life and learn to say no. Let first things come first.

Part III

The Intimacy Factor:
Battle Scars or Blessings?

7

Love Is a Four-Letter Word

The basic ingredient of most marital problems is lack of communication. Every commitment made to God and to one another is put to the test at the level of communication. This is the point of contact between two people, where the man and woman either enjoy their relationship by responding properly or endure it by reacting improperly.

Love and blessing are the two foundations of communication. All forms of communication between husband and wife must include them as basic working principles. The principle of love opens the door to communication in an active sense.

What is the definition of *love*? *Love* is a four-letter word consisting of two consonants—*L* and *V*—two vowels—*O* and *E*—and two fools—you and me! Well, you may not define it in this way, but however you define it, true love was never meant to be passive. After the honeymoon is over, many marriages are hit with the same problem: staleness! The love that once burned with excitement grows cold. It burns out.

A good illustration of this stale relationship is that of the Joneses. Mrs. Jones just wasn't talking much to her husband anymore. So he decided she needed counseling. After nine weeks the counselor was baffled! On the tenth week the desperate counselor asked Mr. Jones to accompany his wife to the session. Once they were seated in the office the counselor stood up, walked around his desk to Mrs. Jones, and kissed her on the cheek. Mrs. Jones instantly began to come alive, hugged her husband, and told him all that had been happening over the past three months. Mr. Jones was shocked! He took the counselor into the other room and said, "I don't understand—what happened?"

"Don't you see," the doctor blurted out, "your wife needs this kind of treatment Monday, Wednesday, and Friday!" Mr. Jones scratched his head in confusion and said, "Well, I can get here on Monday and Wednesday, but I can't make it on Friday." Obviously, Mr. Jones missed the point. The counselor didn't want to administer the treatment—he wanted Mr. Jones to do that!

The little things in life demonstrate love so effectively. I can take my wife out to a nice steak dinner. When it's all over I'll ask, "Did you like it?" Her reply is, "I liked it, but I feel kind of sick. I ate too much." Now I spent all that money to make my wife sick. During the summer months you can buy some flowers for a few dollars on nearly every major street corner. When I pick up a bunch of the flowers and use the old behind-the-back trick at the door, my wife goes into ecstasy. For twenty dollars I make her sick—for a few dollars she is overwhelmed! It's just a sound investment—little things in life demonstrate love best.

Explanation of True Love

There is so much confusion in our world today concerning *love*. Most marital relationships have a wrong picture of love. Have you ever said, "I love oranges"? Exactly what do you mean by that? You are actually saying, "Oranges do something for me." However, after you have squeezed everything you like out of the orange, you throw away the peelings. This is the same concept of love that many take as a basis for marriage. So when a person says *I love you* he or she really means, "You do something for me. After I squeeze all I want out of you, I will discard you, even as I threw away the orange peelings." Now there is nothing wrong with being attracted to the one you love and excited that he or she "does something for you," but that is not a proper foundation for marriage.

True love is not *getting* all you can from another person but *giving* all you can. It is not conditional on what your lover does for you but is totally unconditional. One Greek word for *love* is *agape*, which translated means to commit yourself to seek the best for the object loved. It's committing yourself to give to another. It's a stubborn kind of love. It says, "I love you no matter what you do, say, or how you look. I love you! You can't stop me!"

The most precise and dynamic statement of true love is found in 1 Corinthians 13:4–7:

> Love is patient, love is kind, and is not jealous; love does not brag and is not arrogant, does not act unbecomingly; it does not seek its own, is not provoked, does not take into account a wrong suffered, does not rejoice in unrighteousness, but rejoices with the truth; bears all things, believes all things, hopes all things, endures all things.

Let's look at definitions of each of the terms describing *agape love* and begin to think of the application to marriage. (Be prepared for painful conviction!)

Love is patient.   Love enables you to endure offense from your mate, even though there is a tide of emotion welling up within you demanding that you retaliate. This is the kind of patience that waits, prays for the reformation of your mate, and keeps you from lashing out in resentment against his or her conduct. Love will suffer many slights and neglects from the beloved and wait to see the kindly effects of such patience on him or her.

Love is kind.   It responds with kindness when ill-treated. It seizes on opportunities to demonstrate tenderness and goodwill.

Love is not jealous.   Love is never displeased at the successes or blessings that come to the mate. Envy sprouts from a relationship of competition and comparison.

Love does not brag.   Love never tries to show off and brag about itself. There is no outward display of boasting. Never brag about your strengths in order to magnify your mate's weaknesses: "*I* don't ever have this problem" or "You don't see *me* doing that kind of thing, do you?" To love your mate involves esteeming him or her above yourself.

Love is not arrogant.   Arrogance is an inner attitude of pride that stems from man worship, a knowledge of Scripture apart from application: "superspirituality." One mate should never communicate that the other is "out of it" spiritually. It's so easy to intimidate—love does not do that.

Love does not act unbecomingly.   Love does not behave in an unmannerly way, according to society's dictates of manners. A very simple yet destructive way of behaving unmannerly is to poke fun at or cut your mate down in public—or in private, for that matter!

Love does not seek its own.   Love never seeks for its own interests—only for those of the mate. Be an ardent student of your mate's interests and take some positive action in those areas.

I like all kinds of sports, but there is one I've never even classified as a sport: hiking. I mean, tennis, basketball, and golf are unquestionably great sports. But hiking? It seems so meaningless to me—aimlessly wandering around through the woods. My wife's favorite "sport" happens to be hiking. It's been so difficult to get her interested in something like tennis. But my difficulty was caused by my "seeking my own." One day I woke up to this and said, "Let's go hiking!"

"Hiking?"

"Yeah, let's go out and aimlessly wander through some woods!" (I almost lost my good effort with that last statement.) You know, that small action opened her up to participate in some *genuine* sports activities with me. Love does not seek its own.

Love is not provoked.   It doesn't become bitter or resentful as a result of continuous irritations or offenses and will not respond to offenses with touchiness or anger.

Love does not take into account a wrong suffered.   Love doesn't take evil into account when offended; it doesn't consider evil as a debt owed (something that must be "paid back"), and it never imputes evil motives to others.

Love does not rejoice in unrighteousness. Love never takes pleasure in the misfortunes that befall one's mate; it never has a "serves him right" attitude. You should not reflect an attitude of joy when your mate suffers the consequences of his or her offense or failure—even if you told him so.

Love rejoices in the truth. Love rejoices when truth is clearly presented and feels an inward joy and desire to respond to it. Heated arguments are normally a result of trying to win rather than seeking to find the truth and rejoicing in it. There is one time I don't want to rejoice in the truth—that is when my wife and I disagree, and she's more right than I am. This is the time I put on the righteous airs and say, "We really shouldn't argue about it. That's silly. Let's just drop the subject!" I know, if we continue, she will be proven right. On the other hand, the time I love to rejoice in the truth is when I'm more right than my wife; of course, my motive isn't too righteous in this case.

Love bears all things. Love equips you both to endure offense from your mate and to put a cloak of silence over your sufferings so that your mate's offenses and misdeeds are not divulged to the world. As a ship keeps water out, so love keeps the world from knowing the possible wrongs your mate is committing against you. There are affairs within your marriage that should be kept within the confines of the home. Too often extremely personal marital matters are publicized without discretion in prayer groups, usually under the guise of concern or a prayer request. Each mate must be able to trust in the other.

Love believes all things.   Love chooses to believe the best about the person and always assumes his or her motives and intentions are pure. To trust in your mate gives him or her a feeling of self-worth and acceptance. This is a key to effecting positive changes in the one you love.

Take a single girl named Sally and ask her what she thinks of John. "Oh, John, he's all right. He's just another guy." Then you let it be known that John thinks Sally is a beautiful girl and he really likes her. Now ask Sally the same question about John. Her reply? "Oh, that John, he's got insight!" What pepped up her response? She felt vibrations of love from John and she couldn't help but respond. The same is true of love vibrations in the marital relationship, except in this case it's more of a necessity for oneness.

Love hopes all things.   Love gives you a confident expectation, based on the provision of God, that the offenses committed by your mate will be rectified and his or her weaknesses ultimately will be corrected, even in the face of evidence to the contrary. You should continue to hope joyfully, even in times of discouragement.

Love endures all things.   Patient endurance is the quality that proves love for God. It enables one to endure any trial with a confident and joyful heart, because of the personal discipline that will be developed and the blessing of God that will result. Divorce is not a manifestation of the love that endures all things. The essence of love is commitment!

First Corinthians 13 is referring to a life-style. The fact that all the verbs in this passage are in the present tense emphasizes that these characteristics of love are to be habitually, repeatedly shown. However, just because a person doesn't possess one of these qualities in every instance does not necessarily mean his life-style is contrary to the passage. It's a *process of growth in true love!*

Realizing true love is one thing and releasing true love is quite another.

8

True Love: Release It![1]

In an Asian monastery there were very strict rules. The most unusual restriction was that each monk could only speak two words every ten years.

After Brother Barney had been in residence for ten years, he was brought in to his superior to speak his two words. "All right, Brother Barney, what are your two words?" asked the superior. Brother Barney sheepishly said, "Food, bad!"

At the end of his next ten years Brother Barney was called in for his two-word interview. "What do you have to say for yourself?" Brother Barney meekly murmured, "Bed, hard!"

Now after thirty years he was called in for his third interview. This time Brother Barney angrily blurted out, "I quit!" His superior quickly responded, "Well, I'm not surprised. All you have been doing for thirty years is complaining!"

People are lonely primarily because they are unwilling to communicate to others. Like Brother Barney, people don't say much! Even though there are no monastic restrictions, most of us make only a weak response to the invitation of encountering others because we feel uncomfortable in our nakedness as persons.

Five Levels of Communication

Someone has delineated five levels of communication on which people can relate to one another. Each level represents a different degree of willingness to communicate. We seem to find our comfort zone on one of these levels in every relationship we encounter.[2]

Clichés—Level Five

This level is the lowest level of communication and openness. Communication at this level is accidental, at best. It consists of surface conversation such as, "How are you? . . . It's good to see you! . . . How is your work?" Naturally, nobody really wants an answer to these questions other than a similar surface response.

Actually, it's noncommunication! There is no sharing of personness at all. Everyone remains safely in the isolation of his pretense, sham, sophistication. The whole group seems to gather to be lonely together.

Reporting Facts—Level Four

Communication on this level does not penetrate the surface relationship. It's just that more information is passed back and forth than in the use of clichés. Instead of any self-disclosure there is a reporting on others. Just as we hide behind clichés, so we also hide behind gossip, conversation, and little narrations about others. On this level nothing is given of ourselves and nothing from others is drawn out.

My Thoughts and Judgments—Level Three

At this level there is some communication of personness. Even though we may share ideas, judgments, and decisions, there is strict censorship. As John Powell expresses it:

> As I communicate my ideas, etc; I will be watching you carefully. I want to test the temperature of the water before I leap in. I want to be sure that you will accept me with my ideas, judgments, and decisions. If you raise your eyebrow or narrow your eyes, if you yawn or look at your watch, I will probably retreat to safer ground. I will run for the cover of silence, or change the subject of conversation, or worse, I will start to say things I suspect that you want me to say. I will try to be what pleases you.[3]

My Feelings—Level Two

Level three is a mind boggler! At level two we relate much deeper and much closer to the "real" me! It's a shift from the head to the heart—feelings and emotions. These feelings are uniquely, personally mine. They compose the heart behind my ideas, judgments, and decisions.

Honesty is most difficult at this level! The temptation is to be dishonest on the grounds that it might hurt others. But real growth can take place at this level if communication is honest, open, and gut level.

Intimacy—Level One

Gut-level communication is for complete emotional and personal communion. It's a celebration of intimacy! The celebration of "us"! At this level we share together, care together, laugh and cry together, like two musical instruments playing exactly the same note in unison or in harmony. *It's the miracle of interdependence at its peak!*

Releasing God's Love

The nature of loneliness, like all of our toothaches, centers the focus of attention on ourselves. As we seek to fill this vacuum and to satisfy the hunger of loneliness, we normally do something very stupid. We try to manipulate people into loving us. We know that our loneliness can be relieved by the love of others. We know we must feel loved. The paradox is this: *If we seek to fill the void, we will find no relief but only a deeper vacuum.* We deceive ourselves into believing that our search to be loved is loving. Most of our time and energy is spent on the prowl looking for this experience called love. But the paradox remains: if we seek the love we need, we will never find it![4]

Why is this paradox so real? Because being on the prowl is not love at all. Love can never be captured, bought, or taken. It must always be given away. *You must decide to actively release God's love!*

Plugged into a relationship with God, the source of love and life, you must now turn to developing interdependent relationships on the human level. To release God's love, I suggest six action steps. You release love by . . .

Exposing

Expose yourself! *Tell the truth about yourself.* We resist self-disclosure. We want a place of safety, barricaded against the invasion of others with their probing questions and inquisitive desire to know all about us. There is no nakedness more painful than psychological nakedness. This need for safety and self-protection breeds a deadly myth. The myth is that everyone needs his own private retreat where no one else can enter. It sounds good and is most popular, but it is only an exercise in wishful thinking. Rather than a place reserved exclusively for self, what we really need is to have someone (a total confidant) know us completely and some others (close friends) know us very deeply. The pockets of privacy we create for a place to run where no one can follow are death to the kind of intimacy so necessary to the fullness of life.[5]

In his book *The Transparent Self,* psychologist Sidney Jourard relates some illuminating studies about the subject of self-disclosure. His major finding is that the human personality has a natural, built-in inclination to reveal itself. When that inclination is blocked and we close ourselves to others, we get into emotional difficulties. This is why the most frequent expression heard by the counselor (professional or amateur) is "You are the first person I have ever been completely open and honest with!"[6]

We have the ambivalent feelings of longing to be known and understood on the one hand, and desiring to remain hidden and covered up on the other. Therefore, we build walls between relationships instead of bridges to link relationships together. All the masks of loneliness come to our aid as we run from exposing ourselves.

The brilliant Swiss psychiatrist Carl Jung advised his patients to become acquainted with what he called the "shadow side" of themselves, or the "inferior part of the personality." There is a hidden portion of our minds that is comprised of memories from the past which terrify us and of which we are ashamed, plus the mean, selfish, and base nature which erupts occasionally and which we try to excuse and explain away in a thousand different ways. The natural assumption is that if we let others see this dark side, they will be turned away or even hate us. But generally, they are able to be more empathetic and understanding with us than we are with ourselves. A curious kind of chemistry starts to work. Through telling another person the truth about ourselves, we begin to understand ourselves better. It's the principle of losing yourself in order to find yourself![7]

Two cautions should be heeded as you take the risk of exposing yourself. The first is the extreme of telling the truth about yourself to just *anyone* or to someone special *all at once.* Choose your confidants carefully and expose yourself gradually. The second caution is to tell the truth *about yourself and not about others.* There is a natural tendency, as it becomes easier to open up, to do some "mind reading" and "fortune-telling"—trying to tell what you believe to be the truth about others. You are only responsible for *your* self-disclosure. You cannot self-disclose someone else. It's nothing more than psychological rape!

Emoting

The second action step in releasing love is to express your gut-level emotions. This is emoting!

Emotions are not moral. Both good and bad emotions are okay. They are simply factual and must be reported. Feeling frustrated, or being annoyed, or experiencing fears and anger do not make a person good or bad.

If our emotions are not *reported*, they will be *repressed*. If our censoring consciences do not approve certain emotions, we repress these emotions into our subconscious minds. Experts in psychosomatic medicine say that the most common cause of fatigue and actual sickness is the repression of emotions.[8]

Instead of repressing, report your emotions! If you feel angry, sad, disappointed, or guilty, report these feelings as your feelings. If I am to tell you who I am, I must tell you about my feelings, whether I act upon them or not. I may tell you that I am angry, explaining the fact of my anger without implying any judgment of you, and not intending to act upon this anger. I may tell you that I am afraid, explaining the fact of my fear without accusing you of being its cause, and at the same time not being overwhelmed by the fear. But I must, if I am to expose myself to you, allow you to experience my person and report to you my anger and my fear.[9]

As much as is possible emotions should be reported on the spot—right at the time you are feeling them. The balance of when, how, and *to whom* you report your emotions must be carefully juggled. Count on making mistakes, and when you do, report that emotion as well! This balancing act of properly reporting your feelings as you check in with your mind is all part of processing your emotions instead of dangerously repressing them. When you repress your feelings, you will inevitably pay for it in your stomach!

Be careful not to spill your guts in every relationship. It's impossible to relate to everyone on the most intimate, number-one gut level. All kinds of people may desire a more intimate relationship with you, but you must remain in control. In some ways, it sounds good, even mature, to be able to relate to everyone on the number-one level. To be *able* to relate on that level is mature, but to attempt this with everyone is immature and idealistic. There is no magic number of people for you to include on the number-one level of relationships. But a good guideline is to relate to at least two on this intimate level. Some can handle more than twenty, others feel most comfortable with four or five, but you cannot afford to have less than two!

Judging

It is said that the favorite indoor sport of most churches is confessing the sins of others!

Condemning others, their actions, and feelings, is the exact opposite of the biblical blueprint for true love. Condemnatory judgment expects to find fault and enjoys criticism for its own sake. It's one of the most destructive elements of all as you attempt to release love within a relationship.

So why do I say that by judging you take another step in the act of releasing love? There are two basic definitions of *judgment.* One is "to condemn" as described above. The other is "to conclude"—to esteem, to determine, to think. Only God can condemn someone. But man must make conclusions—he must judge by conclusion! When the conclusion kind of judgment is understood and practiced, relationships become more clarified, honest, and open!

Obviously, since judging in the spirit of conclusion is meant to be an act of love, the whole process of confronting can only happen within the context of a secure love relationship. In other words, when you judge in this way you must be sure to communicate your unconditional love.

David Augsburger, in his practical *Caring Enough to Confront,* encourages confrontation when the proper context exists. Giving another person feedback on how he or she is coming on can be surprisingly simple when it is offered in a context of caring, supportive acceptance; it can be astoundingly difficult when interpreted as insensitive, nonsupportive rejection.

Hearing confrontation from another is no problem when one is certain that the other respects, values, and cares in spite of all differences; but when respect is unclear and caring is unexpressed, one can feel fed up with another's feedback before it even begins.

Caring comes first, confrontation follows. A context of caring can be created when a person is truly *for* another, genuinely *concerned about* another, authentically *related to* another. The context of such caring is, however, not a blank-check approval of the other person. The core of true caring is a clear invitation to grow, to become what he or she truly is and can be, to move toward maturity. Accepting, appreciating, valuing another is an important part of a relationship, but these attitudes may or may not be caring. The crucial element is: Does it foster growth? Does it invite maturing? Does it set another free to be? Is it truly an expression of love?

A context of caring must come before confrontation.
A sense of support must be present before criticism.
An experience of empathy must precede evaluation.
A basis of trust must be laid before one risks advising.
A floor of affirmation must undergird any assertiveness.
A gift of understanding opens the way to disagreeing.
An awareness of love sets us free to level with each other.

Building solidarity in relationships with others—through caring, support, empathy, trust, affirmation, understanding, and love— provides a foundation for the more powerful actions of confrontation, criticism, evaluation, counsel, assertiveness, disagreement, and open leveling with each other.[10]

But why are we to judge, even by conclusion, in our relationships? What does judging have to do with releasing love to another? You see, judging in the right spirit is a critical ingredient in loving. Loving another person always involves face-to-face confrontation. To avoid the pain and uneasiness of confronting in a love relationship is not to love at all! The wise man Solomon put it this way: "An open rebuke is better than love in secret" (*see* Proverbs 27:5).

Caring enough to confront means that you are willing to risk being misunderstood as you admonish, warn, disagree, or rebuke a loved one. A true friend or lover will express his conclusions about you because he loves you. A person who is unwilling to tell you when you have food on your face is not releasing love to you.

The biblical blueprint for judging with the spirit of conclusion has been greatly misunderstood:

> "Do not judge lest you be judged yourselves. For in the way you judge, you will be judged; and by your standard of measure, it will be measured to you. And why do you look at the speck in your brother's eye, but do not notice the log that is in your own eye? Or how can you say to your brother, 'Let me take the speck out of your eye,' and behold, the log is in your own eye? You hypocrite, first take the log out of your own eye, and then you will see clearly enough to take the speck out of your brother's eye."
>
> Matthew 7:1–5

Most people use this section of the biblical blueprint to justify that we are never to judge at all. But it's expressing just the opposite! "Do not judge lest you be judged" is a Hebrew idiom which says that we are to *judge ourselves first.* Judging with the spirit of conclusion demands a proper starting point—start with *you!* When you make a conclusion kind of judgment, you set yourself up as an authority. And as that authority you will be judged by the same standard you use in judging others. It makes sense to start by looking into the mirror.

There are two problems when a conclusion judgment is made improperly. The first is the problem of credibility. How can you look at the speck that is in your brother's eye but not notice the log that is in your own eye? How can you confront a friend about something in his life while you are guilty of the same thing? It's a pretense of being moral and righteous. Without removing the log in your own eye, your action quickly loses credibility!

The second is the problem of effectiveness. How can you say to your brother, "Let me take the tiny speck out of your eye," when you have a large log in your own eye? It's a pretense of being able to help. With that log in your eye you cannot be effective in removing the speck from your brother's eye! You can't see clearly enough to help.

Judging properly includes two simple steps: be a log remover, then be a speck remover! A little girl, visiting her grandmother, was helping out by dusting the dining-room table. When her grandmother inspected the table she said, "That's good, honey, but there is a large area in the middle of the table that you missed!" The little girl redusted the table and announced her accomplishment. Again her grandmother inspected the table: "You still haven't dusted that area right in the middle of the table!" Once more the little girl dusted diligently, and again her grandmother chastised her for her poor dusting job. Exasperated, the little girl realized what was happening. She blurted out, "Grandma, the dust is not on the table. It's on your glasses!" *Be a log remover before you become a speck remover.*

Forgiving

Someone said, "I have forgiven and forgotten, and I don't want you to forget that I have forgiven and forgotten!" That's not pure forgiveness! Because of the various weaknesses and mistakes within people, forgiveness is absolutely necessary for love to be released. When you are wronged or hurt by your loved one, you have a few choices. You can try *retaliation* for the purpose of repayment for your hurt. But repayment is impossible! You can try *revenge*, but revenge is ineffective! Revenge not only lowers you to the level of your "enemy" but it boomerangs as well. The person who seeks revenge is like the man who shoots himself in order to hit his enemy with the kick of the gun's recoil. You can also try *resentment.* But resentment not only hurts others, it hurts *you* even more![11]

There is an interesting dynamic in the act of forgiving. Throughout the biblical blueprint there is a couplet: *Forgive so that you might be forgiven.* Unless you forgive, you will not be forgiven.

The whole package of forgiveness sets you free from the three most basic psychological problems of *fear, anger,* and *guilt.* Experiencing forgiveness through a relationship with God gives the power to eliminate the core problem of fear. On the horizontal, human level, when you forgive you experience freedom from your anger and resentment. And when you are forgiven by another, you are set free from your guilt.

But what is forgiveness? How does it work? Forgiveness begins with a (1) *respect for otherness.* You must give the freedom to your loved one to be different from you. This includes strengths as well as weaknesses. It's the freedom to succeed and the freedom to fail—*the freedom to be.* Then, forgiveness means to (2) *differentiate between your offender and the offense.* It *is* possible to hate the offense and yet love the offender. You must separate the two in order to forgive.

Forgiveness also involves (3) *being willing to hurt in order to heal.* Since repayment is really impractical and most ineffective, someone must bear the hurt. When you choose to forgive, you are also choosing to be the sufferer in order for healing to take place within the relationship. To forgive is to make a heavy love commitment!

To help the healing process, (4) *giving a blessing* is necessary! Giving a blessing can be a gift, but verbalization is most effective. It's genuinely expressing thankfulness and praise for qualities you appreciate in the other person. Love itself is revolutionary, but love's expression through giving a blessing in reaction to a hurt is the most rare of all!

Finally, forgiveness requires (5) *forgetting the offense.* To begin the process of forgiving with trying to forget makes it worse. Forgetting is the *result* of complete forgiveness; it is never the *means.* It is the final step, not the first!

There is no forgiveness in the cheap little game of looking the other way when a wrong is done. Forgiveness never just overlooks or winks at a wrong. It does not make light of the offense. It's no bit of pious pretending that an offense is not really an offense. Forgiveness is not mere politeness, tact, or diplomacy! Nor is it just forgetting. You will forget after you truly forgive. But to insist that forgetting comes first is to make passing the final exam the entrance requirement for the course. The person who struggles to forget without going through the prior steps of forgiveness only sears the thought more deeply into his memory.

Touching

The fifth action step in releasing God's love is to touch! Our society dwells in two extremes. On the one hand, we distance ourselves from people without developing healthy relationships with them. On the other hand, we jump into sexual relationships without a healthy relationship. Some people are paranoid about any physical contact. Others are obsessed with the physical "urge to merge."

Somewhere in between these extremes is the healthy balance. It's learning to release love by touching! Touching is the coup de grace of communications. If you view man as a spiritual, emotional, and physical being, you can appreciate the magnitude of this expression. Touching is the one communication form that ties all three dimensions into one. Because we are in part physical beings, we need to relate to our world through touch from the time of birth. For infants the need for touch is so great that they literally cannot survive without it. Through this sense mechanism early feelings of warmth, security, and comfort begin to grow.[12]

Love released by touching is an act of tenderness and warmth. Loving tenderness is a need all people have, yet in American culture such expression is often discouraged. Grace Stuart explains in a passage from *Narcissus*:

> It is too seldom mentioned that the baby, being quite small for quite a long time, is a handled creature, handled and held. The touch of hands on the body is one of the first and last of physical experiences and we deeply need that it be tender. We want to touch ... and a culture that has placed a taboo on tenderness leaves us stroking our dogs and cats when we may not stroke each other. We want to be touched ... and often we dare not say so. ... We are starved for the laying on of hands.[13]

When counseling children caught in the middle of a divorce, the concept of love released through physical touch is most clear. One of the goals in these cases is to assure the children of their parents' love for them. The counselor's question might be, "You know your dad loves you, don't you?" Invariably the child's response is, "Yeah, my dad wrestles with me!" or "I know, because he tickles me!" or

"He dunks me in the pool!" *Love is magically released and effectively communicated through touching!*

During the nineteenth century more than half of the infants in the United States died in their first year of life from a disease called *marasmus,* a Greek word meaning "wasting away." As late as the 1920s, according to Montagu, the death rate for infants under one year of age in various United States foundling institutions was close to 100 percent! A distinguished New York pediatrician, Dr. Chapin, noted that the infants were kept in sterile, neat, tidy wards, but were rarely picked up. Chapin brought in women to hold the babies, coo to them, and stroke them, and the mortality rate dropped drastically. Just like the babies, millions of lonely people are sick and dying because of a lack of warmth and tenderness— much of it through touch![14]

One caution is appropriate here: *physical gushing is as offensive as verbal gushing.* But when it is a genuine expression of your love, touch may bring you closer to another person than thousands of words can. Men can find masculine ways of giving a loving message to other men. Get into the habit of shaking hands. The act of your going to the person and getting the proximity of your bodies necessary for the handshake conveys a message. A pat on the back, a playful punch in the stomach, "Give me five!" or your hand on a man's shoulder as you talk—all these should make up your vocabulary of gestures. In our contacts with the opposite sex, touching need not always have a sexual connotation. We can give encouragement, offer comfort, or express tenderness with physical demonstrations.[15]

Love by touching communicates, "I affirm you!" or "I care about you!"

Initiating

The final suggested action step for releasing love in a relationship is all-encompassing. It is releasing love by initiating love! We all need love from others, but to be lovable we must be lovers.

This initiation of love cannot be based on the feeling of obligation:

Obligation Says	*Love Says*
I must because I owe it.	I will because I choose to.
I should because it's expected of me.	I want to because I care.
I ought to because I'm supposed to.	I'd like to.[16]

The initiation of love requires that you love yourself first. The biblical blueprint says, "Love your neighbor as yourself!" The corollary to this principle is, "If you don't love yourself, then your neighbor is in a heap of trouble!" Self-love is usually mistaken for selfishness, but they are miles apart. Selfishness is destructive. Self-love is the first step toward initiating love's release. It's interesting that one of the most critical steps in relieving the pain of loneliness is to develop love for oneself all *alone!*

There is a growing consensus of opinion that there is one need so fundamental and so essential that if it is met, everything else will almost certainly harmonize in a general sense of well-being. When this need is properly nourished, the whole human organism will be healthy and the person will be happy. This need is a true and deep love of self, a genuine and joyful self-acceptance, an authentic self-esteem which results in an interior sense of celebration: "It's good to be me—I am very happy to be me!"[17]

Instead of waiting around for the love of others, the decision to release true love calls for your initiation. If you want to feel loved, then love. The power of love is phenomenal when unleashed! That power is so effective that the biblical blueprint even directs the loving of your enemies!

9

Blessings on Your Head

WIFE: "If you were reincarnated, you'd come back as a dog!"
HUSBAND: "Yeah, and it would be just my luck that you'd return as a flea!"

The second foundational principle of the communication process is the principle of *blessing*. Blessing opens the door to communication in a reactive sense. This may be the most radical principle of human relationships. Love is revolutionary, but giving a blessing for an insult is most incompatible with what the human nature automatically wants to do! There is very little written about such a radical response pattern other than in the Bible.

The normal reaction to an insult is to respond with another one—only it must be more cutting. Biblical examples of insults are interesting. You may find your "spiritual gift" in this list:

Name-calling: Acts 23:4
Sarcasm and ridicule: John 9:28
A nagging wife: Proverbs 25:24; 27:15
A contentious man: Proverbs 26:21
Insult and abuse in general: 1 Corinthians 5:11; 6:9, 10

The insulting response will get you nowhere but into miniwarfare! The proper reaction is to respond with a blessing for an insult!

After a lengthy discussion concerning proper conduct within various contexts, Peter uses the principle of blessing to sum up all relationships:

> To sum up, let all be harmonious, sympathetic, brotherly, kindhearted, and humble in spirit; not returning evil for evil, or insult for insult, but giving a blessing instead; for you were called for the very purpose that you might inherit a blessing. For "Let him who means to love life and see good days Refrain his tongue from evil and his lips from speaking guile. And let him turn away from evil and do good; Let him speak peace and pursue it. For the eyes of the Lord are upon the righteous. And His ears attend to their prayer, But the face of the Lord is against those who do evil."
>
> 1 Peter 3:8–12

What is a *blessing?* There are four ways the term is used in the Bible: (1) *The praise of God.* What positive qualities in your mate can you praise? (2) *Benefits—gifts—bestowed.* What benefits can you offer your mate? In what way can you be a blessing to him or her? (3) *Giving thanks to God for His gifts and favor.* What qualities about your mate are you thankful for, and how can you communicate this to him or her? (4) *To call God's favor down upon.* What specific areas of your mate's life should you pray that the Lord will bless? These are the blessings that should be rendered in response to the insults you receive.

The principle of rendering a blessing for an insult is common throughout the New Testament.

> Never pay back evil for evil to anyone. Respect what is right in the sight of all men.
>
> Romans 12:17
>
> See that no one repays another with evil for evil, but always seek after that which is good for one another and for all men.
>
> 1 Thessalonians 5:15
>
> and we toil, working with our own hands; when we are reviled, we bless; when we are persecuted, we endure.
>
> 1 Corinthians 4:12
>
> bless those who curse you, pray for those who mistreat you.
>
> Luke 6:28

"You have heard that it was said, 'You shall love your neighbor, and hate your enemy.' But I say to you, love your enemies, and pray for those who persecute you in order that you may be sons of your Father who is in heaven; for He causes His sun to rise on the evil and the good, and sends rain on the righteous and the unrighteous. For if you love those who love you, what reward have you? Do not even the tax-gatherers do the same? And if you greet your brothers only, what do you do more than others? Do not even the Gentiles do the same?'"

Matthew 5:43–47

Why a Blessing?

Why do we need to give blessings? Why not a "righteous" jab? Rendering a blessing for an insult is far from normal for the average person. However, if God designed the family, He certainly knows what makes it work best.

As always, God doesn't leave us hanging over the edge of a cliff in order to take a leap of faith into the cold darkness. In 1 Peter 3:9, 10, 12, four reasons you should render a blessing are given. First:

". . . for you were called for the very purpose that you might inherit a blessing" (verse 9). The purpose of the Christian life is wrapped up in the desire of God that believers might enjoy the blessings of life. So a believer must give a blessing in order to inherit a blessing.

Second: "Let him who means to love life and see good days Refrain his tongue from evil . . ." (verse 10). The one who gives a blessing instead of an insult will have days free from frustration and tension. Many people are burdened with heaviness brought about by wrong reactions toward others. Bitterness and resentment eat away at people's insides, causing problems ranging from ulcers to death. Giving a blessing lifts that burden!

Third: "For the eyes of the Lord are upon the righteous, And His ears attend to their prayer . . ." (verse 12). The Lord will protect those who give a blessing and will hear their prayers. One might tend to think that giving a blessing affords a perfect opportunity for a person to be taken advantage of. ("I might get stomped on if I gave a blessing!") But the promise of the Lord to the one giving the blessing refutes that idea.

At this point you may be wondering why Peter has failed to mention the responsibilities of the one who is persecuting you. It's intentional! It's more important to God that you learn how to respond to hurt in a godly way than for you to be delivered from the one who is hurting you. God wants us to view these situations as part of a learning experience; instead of seeing them as a prison of circumstances, we are to see them as opportunities to grow to maturity. However, once you have responded the way God wants you to by giving a blessing, God then promises that He will begin to deal with the mate who is hurting you.

Fourth: ". . . But the face of the Lord is against those who do evil" (verse 12). The person who refuses to give a blessing but gives an insult must reckon with the Lord. The Lord will work on him! Paul sheds some light on this concept in Romans:

> Never take your own revenge, beloved, but leave room for the wrath of God, for it is written, "Vengeance is Mine, I will repay, says the Lord." "But if your enemy is hungry, feed him, and if he is thirsty, give him a drink; for in so doing you will heap burning

coals upon his head." Do not be overcome by evil, but overcome evil with good.

Romans 12:19-21

In order for the Lord to work on the one doing evil, you must get out of the way—"leave room for the wrath of God." Let God work on the insulter by your giving a blessing—the Lord will do a much better job than you could ever do. All of this may seem very strange to you, but why not give it a try!

How to Give a Blessing!

Jesus employed four steps in responding to insult, and we are commanded to imitate them. (*See* 1 Peter 2:21–25.)

1. *You are to have no personal offense* (*see* verse 22).   You can't give a blessing to someone if you are the offender! One evening Carol and I had an argument over something. In the midst of it all Carol became quite upset—more than I thought the situation called for. I left the room to allow the scene to cool off. I then returned with a blessing (expressing appreciation for a quality in her life). After I verbalized the blessing, Carol turned and said, "If that was meant to be a blessing, it isn't going to work!" I couldn't be-

lieve it! I said, "What do you mean?" Apparently without realizing
it I cut her with some verbal jab (it's natural for me) while we were
disagreeing. What she was saying was, "If you think you can give a
blessing to me when you were the original offender, you're very
mistaken!" Because I had offended her, I was disqualified in giving
out blessings!

2. *Purpose to render a blessing for the insult or hurt you have experienced* (*see* verse 23).   Here's where the will enters in—decide you are going to give a blessing when insulted. Creatively seek
the appropriate blessing by the use of the following questions:

> What positive elements about my mate can I praise him or her for?
> What benefits could I bestow on my mate?
> In what way can I be a blessing to him or her?
> What qualities about my mate am I thankful for?
> How can I communicate this to him or her?
> What specific areas of my mate's life should I pray that the Lord will
> bless him or her in?

Obviously, the most difficult time to give a blessing is in the heat
of the battle. It's probably better to walk away from the battle, for
both to cool off emotionally. Then return with a genuine blessing.

3. *Commit yourself and the situation to the Lord.*   Thank
Him for raising up this situation for the purpose of developing positive character qualities in your life. Release the Lord to act by giving a blessing!

4. *Purpose to be willing to suffer in order to heal your offender*
(*see* 1 Peter 2:24).   When you give a blessing, all may not be re-
solved for a period of time. In fact, you may look like the fool or be
hurt because of your position of blessing. But for healing to take
place, you just might have to bear the brunt of the pain.

One woman faced with some of the worst insults I've ever wit-
nessed gave some of the best blessings ever given. Her husband
traveled nationally as a salesman. He came home eight to twelve
days per month. He told her he came home only for sex with her;
but in the same breath he related to her his various sexual exploits

around the country. He even mentioned these other women in front of the children. It was a tragic scene! No one would have faulted her for filing for divorce. But someone got to this woman before she did anything drastic and challenged her to heal her mate through being a blessing. It was a real test of how much she loved him. After three long years, he came home for good. Now the family is back together, better than ever before. Was it tough? It was hell on earth! Was it worth it? They couldn't be happier!

When you add *blessing* to the principle of *love*, you have a "dynamic duo" which will overwhelm anyone! A very frustrated and lonely woman came in for counseling. She complained about her husband, who never stayed home. He went to five parties a week, from which he repeatedly came home drunk—the other two nights he worked! I discussed with her how she could allow the Lord to work on him through love and blessing. I also suggested that she go to a party with him. "And get drunk?" she said. "No, just go to the party!" When he arrived home that night he almost went into shock; she was dressed beautifully. He said, "You don't want to go to the party tonight, do you?"

"Yes, I'd like to." (That was his second shock!) They went to the party, and neither of them even had anything to drink. They just sat and talked to each other. When they went to bed that evening, they began to make love. He stopped all of a sudden and asked, "What have you been doing?" She proceeded to tell him, but he stopped her and said, "Never mind, just keep it up, I like it!" A week later she called me and ecstatically said, "He's only been to two parties this week. I went with him to both of them, and he didn't get drunk. He talked to me. The rest of the week he's been home in the evenings talking to me! Can you believe it?" Caught up in her excitement I said, "I can't believe it!"

When your mate insults you, don't retaliate with an insult. Render a blessing, and let God deal with your mate—He'll do a much better job!

10

Spiritual Intimacy

Communication involves something more than words! Each word that is spoken conveys a certain disposition through tonal quality or facial and physical gestures. Words may not even be necessary for a mood or disposition to be recognized. What we call *disposition* the Bible calls *spirit*. The spirit of a person communicates more than most people realize, which is the reason for the biblical warning to "take heed then, to your spirit, and let no one deal treacherously" with his mate (Malachi 2:15). There are certain things about your mate's spirit that can really tick you off. In the process of communication, it's crucial that you pay attention to your spirit and the spirit of your mate. Otherwise, you can have a real mess on your hands!

Spiritual intimacy is the adhesive of marital oneness.

Formation of the Human Spirit

It's interesting to examine the spirit of a person. There are four dimensions of the spirit that specifically relate to the marriage relationship. The first is *mood*. This is by far the most common biblical usage of the word *spirit*. A mood is a pervading disposition or emotional feeling. It refers to a frame of mind or a state of feeling. The spirit of Christmas is the mood of the Christmas season. The Bible speaks of the moods of the human spirit under various categories: a wounded spirit, a revived spirit, a hardened spirit, an upright spirit, and others.

The second dimension of the human spirit is *motivation*. It's within this that you find motivational drives, desires, and goals. This is the seat of proper and improper motives.

The third dimension of the human spirit is *perception*. Perception is how you view life and people. You can view life from God's perspective or from man's perspective. If you view a person from man's perspective, he will be a threat to you. If you view him from God's perspective, you'll see a person with needs which must be met. Perception is also the ability to sense another's spirit. It's a sensitivity or an insensitivity to your mate.

The fourth dimension of the human spirit is *contact with God*. It is in the spirit of a person that he or she either has contact with God or a lack of contact with God. Contact with God affects perception, whether you view life from God's perspective or man's perspective. In turn, how you perceive life directly affects motivation—your goals, motives, and desires. All of these flow into the mood—the disposition of a person.

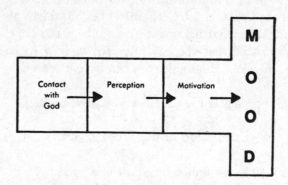

How Spiritual Intimacy Is Broken

There are two ways by which spiritual communication is broken. First, you can have a breakdown in one of the four dimensions of the spirit. There can be a breakdown in contact with God, which short-circuits spiritual intimacy between the partners. This is why many counselors feel it is vital that a couple go to the same church. However, spiritual intimacy does not happen by going into the same building together but by each partner having contact with God.

A breakdown in perception occurs when one mate is insensitive to the other. Quite often I have counseled men who say, "I don't have the foggiest notion why my wife just packed up and left me." I usually reply, "The reason she left is that you haven't had the foggiest notion about much of anything concerning her for a long time." He's lacking in perception as it relates to her.

There can also be a breakdown in the area of motivation. One person may have contact with God and say, "Let's give more money to the church." The mate without contact with God might reply, "The ten dollars we gave last year was entirely too much!" That's a breakdown in the area of communication—goals and desires.

Finally, there can be a breakdown in the area of the mood. The way things are said and the way things are not said can definitely cause a breakdown in communication.

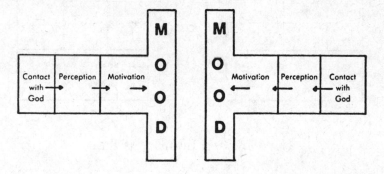

Not only is spiritual communication fractured by a breakdown in the dimensions of the spirit itself but also through a breakdown of specific attitudes. There are at least four attitudes which have significant power in causing disintegration in communication: *nonacceptance, irresponsibility,* an *insulting attitude,* and *selfishness.*

The attitude of nonacceptance will affect the mood negatively. After you express something that is meaningful or exciting to you, nonacceptance might raise its head and respond, "That's ridiculous. Did you think before you said that?" You have just successfully killed communication. The attitude of irresponsibility is present when there is confusion of the roles, or role reversal. The result is competition and a vying for the position of authority, both of which work wonders for the spirit of a relationship! The insulting attitude borders on guerrilla warfare! It constantly gnaws away at the relationship and especially is a hindrance to oneness. The attitude of being selfish—the big "I" problem—destroys two-way communication because everything must revolve around one person. Selfishness drives a person to seek his or her own interests above those of the person he loves.

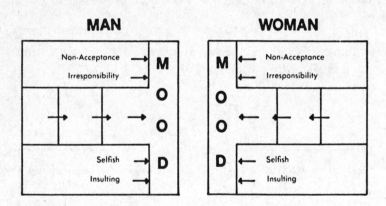

How Spiritual Intimacy Is Built

1. *Establish contact with God.*   A lot of defeat and frustration has greeted couples who try to develop their relationship with God.

My wife and I have tried nearly everything and failed at most attempts. In my first year of seminary I realized that Carol wasn't getting all the fantastic "gems" that I was enjoying, so I decided to set up Timmons Theological Seminary. I could teach her a course each semester over the four years, and she would be the most educated seminary wife ever. We were to meet three times a week for two hours. I determined that the first course was going to be dynamic, so I began with a study of the two most difficult books in the Bible—Daniel and Revelation. I just knew she was going to be totally overwhelmed by my presentation. In the first hour I did an overview of Daniel. The response was not entirely what I anticipated: she yawned and kept looking at her watch. After the overview, we took a ten-minute break, but after about fifteen minutes she hadn't returned. When I finally found her, busily folding clothes, she said, "Oh, is the break over already?" I then did an overview of Revelation. The response was worse than it was for Daniel. Timmons Theological Seminary folded that day.

We tried lots of things to develop our relationship with God. One time we bought some tapes by a man thought to be quite an intellectual. I figured that we really needed what he had to say. Let me make one thing clear: I never fall asleep unless I'm supposed to. I don't fall asleep in class or in meetings because I'm afraid I'll miss something. But this speaker had some rare abilities. I was sitting on the floor against the bed, and Carol was lying on the bed while the tape was playing. All of a sudden I awoke, realizing that I had slept through half of the tape. I was so embarrassed, I turned around quickly to see if Carol had been watching me. She was out cold! I woke her up and we both felt a bit foolish about the whole deal. I asked her what she thought we should do and she said, "Well, maybe we could let the guy put us the rest of the way to sleep." And we did. If you listen to tapes together, be sure that they are the kind that can keep you awake.

One time we decided we wanted to pray together. We didn't know all the fancy words, but we did know that we wanted to talk to God. Our work at that time was bringing us into contact with people who had a lot of problems. So we decided we would pray an hour a day, at half-past six in the morning. The first morning we started praying right on time; we prayed and prayed and prayed.

We looked at the clock. It was 6:40 A.M. We went back to bed. That experience fizzled out after only three mornings.

You must cultivate contact with God together. Let me tell you two things that will work. First, make sure your time together is *short*. You can always extend it. The problem is that we get psyched up over all these great ideas (reading together a chapter a day out of the Book of Proverbs, praying together, and so forth) and fail to see the potential conflicts that come up when everyday problems and interruptions occur. Discouragement sets in! A built-in fizzle takes place when our expectations are unrealistic.

A second sensible step toward establishing a meaningful time together is to make it *regular*. Regular doesn't necessarily mean daily or even every other day. Regular could mean weekly or even an extended time each month, though I think once a year is taking advantage of the principle. Set a regular time together which you can generally control and guard. Carol and I have found that one night per week is best for us. Virtually nothing can interrupt that evening together. If, in a rare case, that night must be canceled, another night in the same week is scheduled.

2. *Build perception—walk in your mate's shoes.*   As we saw earlier, men and women are very different varieties of people. Women are weird and men are strange. In order to unite these two weird-strange people into one spirit, you must identify your mate's difference and actually walk in his or her shoes.

Men are basically physical and women are basically emotional. That doesn't mean that neither of them thinks; nor does it mean that women are not physical, or that men are not emotional. The most intimate door of communication with the man is physical and with the woman it is emotional. If a man wants to open up his wife most intimately, he must relate to her through the emotions—empathizing with her, treating her warmly and tenderly, and genuinely caring for her. This is why unusual things sometimes happen between women with marital problems and their male counselors. That counselor is listening and empathizing with that woman and encouraging her to open up. Perhaps he is the first man in years who has really cared about her. Pretty soon she falls in love with him because he has opened up the most intimate door of her life.

If a woman desires to open up to her husband most intimately she must relate to him physically—sexually.

A lady walked into my office and announced, "I've only got three more weeks, and then my marriage is over!" Her husband had told her in December that he would be leaving at the end of January. He declined to give any reasons. In fact, he clammed up after his announcement and retreated into a shell. She asked what I thought she should do.

"Well," I said, "I have some ideas, but I don't think you can carry them out."

She asked me what I meant by that, and I told her I wasn't the one to help her.

She said, "I've never heard anything like this before in my life. I come in for counseling, you act as if you know the answer, but you aren't going to tell me."

"Well you can't do it," I replied. "Believe me lady, I've dealt with a lot of women in this situation and I know them when I see them. You couldn't do this."

She got upset and blasted back, "Now, look! I'm willing to do *anything* to get my husband back and then to keep him there."

"All right," I said, "I think you're ready. What you need to do is to go home tonight and overwhelm that man sexually."

"Who, me?" she asked in amazement.

"Do you have anybody else in mind?" I asked. "What do you mean, 'me'? Of course, you!"

"Well, I've never done that before," she replied.

I was quick to pounce. "I knew it. Now you are going to feel guilty because you knew what to do and didn't do it."

"I'll do it," she shot back.

The next day she called me. "You won't believe what happened last night," she said.

"What *kind* of happened, generally?" I stuttered. (If you don't screen it right there, you get the whole nine yards.)

She went on. "He actually began to open up last night. There is something wrong at his office, but he didn't explain the entire situation. At least I know it's not just the home situation he's running from. What do you think I should do now?" she asked.

"What do I think you should do now? Again, lady, again!" I said.

Three days later she called me. She went bananas and said, "He told me everything! We talked it all out; I even offered a solution to the problem at the office, which he thought was the answer he needed. We've never had a better talk in thirteen years of marriage!"

3. *Effect changes in your mate through motivation.*   You need to counteract any of the bad attitudes which may have hindered communication with new goals and commitments. (1) To counteract nonacceptance make a commitment to the oneness factor. (2) To counteract irresponsibility make a commitment to the responsibility factor. (3) To counteract selfishness and an insulting attitude make a commitment to the intimacy factor.

Do you see what's happening? The game plan for a maximum marriage is all fitting together to produce an intimate and enjoyable oneness! Your spirits can experience a union through making these basic commitments to your mate—no matter what your mate does or doesn't do.

4. *Attend to your mood.*   You establish spiritual intimacy as you pay attention to your mood and the mood of your mate. Instead of wounding your mate's spirit, try reviving it. The Book of Proverbs has much to say concerning mood as it relates to communication:

> A soothing tongue is a tree of life,
> But perversion in it crushes the spirit.
> Proverbs 15:4
>
> A joyful heart is good medicine,
> But a broken spirit dries up the bones.
> Proverbs 17:22

The Bible speaks of three principles concerning mood in communication: *quick to hear, slow to speak,* and *slow to anger.*

Be Quick to Hear

Listening involves shutting your mouth!   You cannot hear when your mouth is in gear. So many times we fail to listen. Oh, yes, we shake our heads and say, "Hmmm . . ." but we don't listen. Listening is very therapeutic. That's why a person can go to a counselor who does little but listen and feel straightened out after six months. As Proverbs 10:19 says, "When there are many words, transgression is unavoidable, But he who restrains his lips is wise."

Create a nonthreatening climate.   A threatening climate is easily created, even without words. A look or gesture that communicates rejection is a good way to mess up spiritual intimacy.

Empathize, don't sympathize.   Seek to understand the feelings rather than the words. To sympathize is to pat your mate on the back and feel sorry for him or her. To empathize is to identify with his or her feelings by becoming personally involved in them.

Ask questions for clarification.   In the process of listening, you may need to ask a question to be certain you understand. You might say, "You mean . . ." but don't say, "You don't mean. . . ." Demonstrate openness as you inquire.

Be Slow to Speak

Keep communication lines open.   Whenever you feel tension in your communication you can dissolve it by laughing at yourself, verbalizing appreciation, projecting genuine concern, and asking meaningful questions. Normally the husband will come home in the evening and his wife will ask, "What did you do today, honey?" His response is, "Oh, I was at the office. What did you do?" "I was here at the house," she replies. That kind of dynamic interchange can embalm a whole evening. Try asking creative questions.

Avoid explosive words like always *and* never.   The wife may say, "You never come home on time for dinner!" She is saying that her husband has never, not even once, been home for dinner on time. But he's thinking of the one night he did come home on time. The argument begins.

Avoid interrupting your mate or using sarcasm and ridicule.   These do absolutely nothing but stir up anger. "A gentle answer turns away wrath, But a harsh word stirs up anger" (Proverbs 15:1).

Avoid the "you have the same problem" reaction.   When one mate accuses the other of some irresponsibility, the one accused usually refuses to discuss the charge. Instead, he or she turns it back on the accuser and says, "But you are just as irresponsible in this other area when you . . . ." In this situation the real issues are not discussed at all. The couple just keeps score. No one really wants to win—just to keep the score even!

I'm a "Tab-aholic." There's only one problem with being a Tab-aholic—Tab bottles are left in the car, and bottles roll! Carol can't stand the rolling of bottles in the car, so my job is to keep the car free of Tab bottles. My kids are "raisin freaks." They get these little boxes of raisins and they pop them in their mouths all the time. That's fine, except they miss their mouths often, and the backseat of the car is speckled with raisins. Businessmen don't get excited about riding in my backseat, so it is my wife's job to keep the backseat free of raisins.

One evening we were off to some friends' house for dinner. I was waiting in the car listening to the news when I spotted it—a Tab bottle on the floor behind Carol's seat. Instead of removing it, I quickly wrapped a cloth around it and lodged it under her seat so it wouldn't move.

We were running late, so I wasn't wasting any time scooting across intersections. All of a sudden a green light turned red without changing to yellow. I slammed on the brakes and that stupid bottle worked itself loose, flew up, and hit Carol's foot. Carol didn't say a word. She just looked at me. Her spirit did the communicating and it said, *A bottle just hit my foot and you know that you are supposed to take those out of this car!* Instead of admitting my oversight, I turned around and looked in the backseat and said, "I noticed there are still some raisins on the backseat."

Be careful of the "you have the same problem" reaction!

Be Slow to Anger

Your motivation should not be to win but to gain understanding. "He who restrains his words has knowledge, And he who has a cool spirit is a man of understanding" (Proverbs 17:27).

There is nothing wrong with true argument. The freedom to disagree is important. However, the purpose is to come to the true and proper understanding of a given issue. Most arguments in the home stem from competition and comparison. Therefore, each person is out to gain a victory—to win points. This is a futile exercise that constantly hacks away at the oneness of the relationship. Try to stop each other and have each one state the other's argument.

Keep emotions under control. Arguments become quarrels when there is more heat (emotional) than light (understanding). Keep your voice down. Shouting encourages extreme emotional reaction without reflection on what is being said. Another way to trigger emotions is by any short, quick movements—for example, standing quickly and shoving the chair under the table. These quick movements stir up the emotions of your mate. Normally the mate will be moved to shouting. The shouting seems to indicate the one who lost control first, but in truth, it's the one who triggered the shouting with short, quick movements of anger. When I'm in the car and I get upset, I show my anger by stomping on the accelerator. I only recommend this method for those who own economy cars. Short, jerky motions stir up anger.

Make things right before sundown.   Settle all arguments—at least to the point of agreeing to disagree—before going to bed. Too many couples carry the tension and frustration with them to bed and build up resentment that is not dealt with until an explosion occurs much later.

Spiritual intimacy is essential to oneness in marriage. It's just good strategy to strive for spiritual oneness by paying attention to your mate's spirit and to your own.

A husband attended a seminar luncheon at which the speaker lectured on marriage. He was so convinced by the speaker's message that he moved into instant application. He bought flowers, candy, and jewelry and went home early to present them to his wife.

He presented each gift with a kiss and an appropriate word of love. His wife was overwhelmed! She began to cry hysterically and exclaimed, "It's so horrible! It's terrible! It's just terrible!"

Through her tears she explained, "The sink stopped up, the toilet overflowed, our dog was run over, Johnny broke his leg, and now you've come home drunk!"

How about getting drunk on marital spirits? Cultivate your spiritual intimacy with your mate and develop a maximum marriage.

11

The Urge to Merge!

Physical communication is the most intimate expression of a maximum marriage. Statistical studies repeatedly indicate that 75 to 80 percent of marital difficulties can be attributed to sexual problems. Although people are experiencing sexual problems in their marriages, the real causes are much deeper than the physical. I want to open up these nonphysical problem areas and give positive instruction toward physical fulfillment.

Sex is not the key to marital happiness, but it is its most full expression. Nevertheless, problems arise within that expression because of misunderstanding resulting from the lack of positive, directive teaching on the subject. We live in a sex-saturated society. You can hardly buy a can of prunes today without being bombarded by our preoccupation with sex. Much of what our kids learn about sex is picked up from questionable sources and is usually replete with bogus information. Mom and Dad should be the ones doing the instructing in sex education, but too often they have let the schools take the responsibility for educating Junior about sex, and then they resent the way the school goes about it! Parents can give the impression that sex is a dirty subject that is never to be discussed.

Sex is good. As I mentioned earlier, the Bible does not condemn sex by saying, "Thou shalt not." Actually, the Bible says, "Thou shalt, and furthermore, thou shalt enjoy it when thou shalt." Sex is not just for having babies. Most importantly, it is designed to give pleasure, identity, and oneness to the relationship. When sex is viewed purely as the performance of a mechanical, physical act, it quickly begins to rob each partner of the fulfillment and pleasure that it is designed to bring.

The best illustration of the role of sexual love in marriage is found in a book in the Old Testament called the Song of Solomon. The Song of Solomon is a series of reflections by a woman named Shulamit, the wife of Solomon, king of Israel. She reflects about her courtship with Solomon, her wedding day, their first night together, and their later sexual adjustments. Throughout the book, various symbols are used to show sexual desirability and sexual stimulation. Many symbols of speech are used which carry cultural overtones for their time, and I wouldn't suggest using them on your mate. (You might get a violent reaction when you tell your wife, "Your belly is like a heap of wheat.")

Solomon was Israel's richest king. He owned vineyards all over Israel and Syria. While visiting some of his vineyards in northern Israel one day, he met a country girl named Shulamit. Solomon went bananas over this woman, and subsequently visited her several times. Finally he asked her to marry him. Shulamit accepted, but only after serious consideration as to whether or not she really loved him and could be happy in the palace of a king.

Solomon sent a wedding procession to bring his new bride to the palace in Jerusalem, and the book opens as she is getting ready for the wedding banquet and the wedding night. The details of their first night are intimately but tastefully described.

The second half of the book deals with the ups and downs of their married life. One night Solomon makes a play for his wife, but she is not at all interested. He gives her a line of flattery a mile long, and she tells him to forget it! But Solomon returns and they end the evening by making love.

While she lived at the palace, the new queen often longed for the Lebanon mountains in which she was raised. She finally asked Sol-

omon to take her there for a vacation and Solomon agreed. The
book ends with Solomon and Shulamit making love all over the
mountains of Lebanon! Anyone who thinks that God is down on sex
has definitely not read this book!

We take up the story in chapter 1 of the Song of Solomon, which
talks of the *sexual connection*—the bond or trust that creates the
potential for a beautiful relationship. We're not talking only of the
need to *make* a commitment but of the fact of *being* committed.
Lots of people get excited about making a commitment, but few
act as if they *are* committed.

Let's listen to Shulamit as she opens the first section of the Song
of Solomon (1:5, 6):

SHULAMIT: I am black but lovely,
           O daughters of Jerusalem,
           Like the tents of Kedar,
           Like the curtains of Solomon.
           Do not stare at me because I am swarthy,
           For the sun has burned me.
           My mother's sons were angry with me;
           They made me caretaker of the vineyards,
           But I have not taken care of my own vineyard.

This is the first of many portions of the book that deals with sexual identity in symbolism. Shulamit is saying that she has taken care
of the vineyards in the Galilean countryside but she has not done
too well in taking care of her own vineyard—that is, her own sexual
development and external beauty. She has some real questions
about her own desirability and sexual identity.

Next we go to Solomon, who is checking out his new wife at their
wedding banquet (1:9):

SOLOMON: To me, my darling, you are like
          My mare among the chariots of Pharaoh.

It doesn't sound as if Solomon is too swift with words. But Shulamit isn't offended because this was a high compliment in that cul-

ture. The horse was a cherished companion of kings, not a beast of burden.

SOLOMON: Your cheeks are lovely with ornaments,
Your neck with strings of beads.

SHULAMIT: While the king was at his table,
My perfume gave forth its fragrance.

She is saying that Solomon brings out the best in her.

SHULAMIT: My beloved is to me a pouch of myrrh
Which lies all night between my breasts.

This refers to an oriental custom in which a woman would wear a pouch of perfume around her neck all night so that she would smell nice the next day. Shulamit is saying that Solomon is to her like that pouch of myrrh. She says that whatever beauty and charm she has is brought out by her lover. His love causes a fragrance to emit from her all day.

SHULAMIT: My beloved is to me a cluster of henna blossoms
In the vineyards of Engedi.

Across from the Dead Sea in Israel is Engedi. The whole region around Engedi is a very desolate, desert-type area. But as you climb up a small hillside toward Engedi you come upon a lush spring, full of beautiful henna blossoms. Shulamit is saying that Solomon is to her like the ornamental henna blossoms in contrast to the desolate area roundabout. He stands out like that and therefore makes her stand out beautifully.

Later that evening, in the bridal chamber, they continue to express their love (1:15–17):

SOLOMON: How beautiful you are, my darling,
How beautiful you are!
Your eyes are like doves.

SHULAMIT How handsome you are, my beloved,
And so pleasant!
Indeed, our couch is luxuriant!
The beams of our houses are cedars,
Our rafters, cypresses.

She is excited about the way Solomon had the bedroom decorated for her—cedars of Lebanon, cypresses. You know what the most unromantic room in most houses is? The bedroom! Some of us have bedrooms that look like a rock concert just took place in them. Your bedroom should not look like one big closet. Get rid of the spotlight in the middle of the room. Why not try candlelight? Everyone looks better by candlelight!

The story continues in chapter 2 (verse 1):

SHULAMIT: I am the rose of sharon,
The lily of the valleys.

She explains why she is so appreciative of Solomon's efforts to make their bedroom like the countryside which she loves. She says that she is just like a common meadow flower—she has real fears that she is out of place in Solomon's palace.

SOLOMON: Like a lily among the thorns,
So is my darling among the maidens.

Solomon is really turning on the compliments here (2:1). He says that compared to her, all the other girls in the kingdom are as thorns.

SHULAMIT: Like an apple tree among the trees of the forest,
So is my beloved among the young men.
In his shade I took great delight and sat down,
And his fruit was sweet to my taste.

They are apparently actively involved in lovemaking at this point (2:3). The apple (and the symbol of fruit) is a frequent symbol in the Near East for love. It's used throughout the Song of Solomon to denote sexual love. Shulamit is telling Solomon what a good lover he is and how sexually desirable he is to her. She enjoys making love with Solomon!

Sex Is More Than Physical

There's a very simple principle that is being communicated here. When you see someone coming toward you, nine times out of ten there's a person inside that body. (I say nine times out of ten because I've met some strange bodies that made me wonder.) People live in bodies. To prepare for sex by undressing and jumping into bed is to prepare *only* the body. But there is a live person in there who needs attention! The *sexual connection* means you understand that you make love to a person, not a body.

Develop the freedom to verbalize specific instructions. Shulamit gives specific instructions to Solomon as to what she would like him to do in their lovemaking (2:4–6):

SHULAMIT: He has brought me to his banquet hall,
And his banner over me is love.
Sustain me with raisin cakes,
Refresh me with apples,
Because I am lovesick.
Let his left hand be under my head
And his right hand embrace me.

Notice that all of her instructions are positive. When one mate is trying hard to please the other, comments such as "Don't do that!" are not encouraging. Be more positive! Communicate pleasure and enjoyment with positive instructions: "Do this," or "Touch me here."

Are you excited and satisfied with the person who lives inside your mate's body? It will make all the difference in the world whether you enjoy sexual fulfillment in your marriage. There must be a mind-set—not on sex but on the person—not on sexual performance but on giving pleasure! The sexual connection is that of two people, not of two bodies.

The second section of the Song of Solomon deals with *sexual captivation*—two people totally focused on one another.

Masters and Johnson, in their book *The Pleasure Bond*, describe a sexual cycle that many people go through which results in two people being repulsed by sex instead of excited by it. In the first stage, the couple makes a verbal commitment to each other. They sign a piece of paper and figure that the rest is downhill. But they very quickly realize that there is a big difference between making a commitment and being committed to each other. As the couple fail to focus on the needs of each other, their initial verbal commitment is unable to make up for their daily inability to act out their commitment. They then move into stage three, which is where each partner begins to lose his or her security as sexual beings. In counseling I can usually spot a man who is not functioning sexually in marriage because he is not a confident person. He doesn't have a sense of security and he is disintegrating on the inside. Each partner no longer feels uniquely related to the other, nor are they committed to completing each other. They begin to shoot verbally at each other and resent the fact that they are not being cherished.

The final step of disintegration occurs after both partners have met with rejection and defeat—they then become repulsed by the idea of having sex with each other. Sometimes people in this cycle still claim that they have a great sex life, when in reality they have only learned how to use their partners' bodies for ten minutes of satisfaction. That type of sexual relationship does not cultivate intimacy.

Sex Requires Verbalization

For maximum sexual enjoyment your relationship needs the verbal reassurance and affirmation of love. Let's listen in on Solomon and Shulamit on their wedding night (4:1):

SOLOMON: How beautiful you are, my darling,
How beautiful you are!
Your eyes are like doves behind your veil;
Your hair is like a flock of goats
That have descended from Mount Gilead.

Here he goes again! Her "hair is like a flock of goats." He's saying that her hair is long, black, and flowing like a flock of goats as they descend the mountain.

SOLOMON: Your teeth are like a flock of newly shorn ewes
Which have come up from their washing . . .

He's saying that her teeth are beautifully white (4:2). Now some of you won't be able to take the next phrase:

. . . All of which bear twins,
And not one among them has lost her young.

All of her teeth are twins; they come in pairs, top and bottom, and are evenly matched. Not only that, but she still has all her teeth (has lost none of "her young." That could be a little tough on some people. During a marriage seminar a woman came up to me and said, "I've got all my teeth; they're just in a jar at home!")

SOLOMON: Your lips are like a scarlet thread,
And your mouth is lovely.
Your temples are like a slice of a pomegranate
Behind your veil.
Your neck is like the tower of David
Built with rows of stones,
On which are hung a thousand shields,
All the round shields of the mighty men.

Her queenly stature speaks to him of inner strength (4:3, 4). She holds herself well.

Your two breasts are like two fawns,
Twins of a gazelle,

Which feed among the lilies.
Until the cool of the day
When the shadows flee away,
I will go my way to the mountain of myrrh
And to the hill of frankincense.
You are altogether beautiful, my darling,
And there is no blemish in you.

Here they are moving toward consummating their love for each other (4:5–7). I'll tell you one thing: After Solomon got through praising and building up Shulamit, he had one responsive woman on his hands! She may have had a self-image problem before, but she didn't now!

The third section of the Song of Solomon deals with *sexual completion*. What we're really talking about here is body ownership. The Book of 1 Corinthians has something very pertinent to say about this (7:3, 4):

Let the husband fulfill his duty to his wife, and likewise also the wife to her husband. The wife does not have authority over her own body, but the husband does; and likewise also the husband does not have authority over his own body, but the wife does.

Carol and I have had lots of fun with this. I say, "Body [which is her body, but I own it] come here!" She says, "Body [which is my body, but she owns it] go into the kitchen!" You could never get together that way! First Corinthians continues, "Stop depriving one another, except by agreement for a time . . . (7:5).

The Bible is saying something very wise about sex in marriage: learn to meet your mate's sexual needs. Your fulfillment will come not as you satisfy your needs but as you seek to meet your mate's needs in all areas, including the sexual dimension.

The issue is not how often you make love, but that you are always ready to please your mate. I'll never forget sitting in a seminar where the speaker gave the "national average" of lovemaking per week. After he gave it, couples looked at each other in utter amazement. Some felt as if they were hyper and others checked their pulses to see if they were still alive. The so-called national average has nothing to do with your relationship. The real importance is that you're meeting each other's needs sexually.

Now, when you really don't feel like making love with your mate, meet your mate's needs by anticipation. There are certainly genuine reasons for not making love. When I finish speaking at a Maximum Marriage seminar, I'm too tired to pucker, let alone make love. Let's say your wife wants to make love some evening and you really don't feel like it. Here's what you do. Tell her, "Honey, I'll tell you what. Let's make tomorrow night special. You may find this hard to believe, but I will function as head during the valley of the shadow tomorrow; we'll get the kids to bed early, and then we'll be alone to enjoy each other."

The next morning as you leave for work, give her a kiss—not a peck on the cheek, but a real kiss—one that says, *I wish I didn't have to leave you.* Then rush off to work. (That's important!) That afternoon give your wife a call and express your enthusiasm about your coming evening together. You might just call and say two words: *Tonight. Tonight.* One word of caution: Be sure it is your wife who answers the phone. One time a neighbor of ours was visiting Carol when I called. The neighbor answered the phone and I laid on those two words. Carol asked, "Who was it?" Her friend replied, "Well somebody just said, 'Tonight. Tonight,' and hung up. I guess some nut got his jollies for the day." Make sure your wife answers the phone when you pull this off!

Pick up some flowers on the way home—maybe one for each of the years you've known her. (For some people that could get expensive—divide by three.) When you are finally alone, you will not believe the incredible response from your wife. Why? Because you built her mind-set through anticipation.

Be careful of lame excuses. Solomon came to Shulamit's door late at night, wanting to make love. In this case "the king" really did arrive home; but he made the same move men have been famous for making for centuries: the late-night approach. Although his timing was wrong, Shulamit's excuses wouldn't win any awards either (5:2, 3):

SOLOMON: Open to me, my sister, my darling,
My dove, my perfect one!
For my head is drenched with dew,
My locks with the damp of the night.

SHULAMIT: I have taken off my dress,
How can I put it on again?

Can you imagine this poor guy on the other side of the door? He has just given some of his best lines, and his new bride is worried about putting her dress on. He is probably thinking, *So why do you need to put a dress on? What do you think I'm here for, a counseling session?*

SHULAMIT: I have washed my feet,
How can I dirty them again?

Now she's getting religious on him! People in that time practiced a religious ceremony in which they washed their feet before going to bed. Both of her excuses are weak!

One husband in our time wrote to his wife in jest, surfacing the issue of rejection through lame excuses:

To my loving wife,
During the past year I have tried to make love to you 365 times. I have succeeded only 36 times; this is an average of once every 10 days. The following is a list of reasons I did not succeed more often: It was too late—23 times; it will awaken the children—27 times; it's too early—15 times; it's too hot—16 times; it's too cold—5 times; pretending to be asleep—46 times; windows open so that neighbors might hear—9 times; backache—26 times; headache—18 times; toothache—13 times; you had the giggles—6 times; not in the mood—36 times; too full—10 times; baby is crying—17 times; you watched the late TV show—17 times; I watched the late TV show—5 times; mud pack—11 times; company in the next room—11 times; had to go to the bathroom—19 times. That comes to a total of 329 times.

During the times I did succeed, the activity was not entirely satisfactory due to the following: 6 times you chewed gum the whole time; 7 times you watched TV the whole time; 16 times you told me to hurry up and get it over with; 6 times I tried to wake you to tell you we were through; and 1 time I was afraid I had hurt you, for I felt you move.

Honey, it's no wonder I drink too much.

Your loving husband

You are responsible for meeting your mate's needs sexually. Be aware of lame excuses. But meeting your mate's sexual needs may not mean just making love. It may mean showing affection verbally and physically at times other than in bed.

Let's look in at Shulamit as she verbalizes her love and excitement for Solomon (5:10–14):

SHULAMIT: My beloved is dazzling and ruddy,
Outstanding among ten thousand.
His head is like gold, pure gold;
His locks are like clusters of dates,
And black as a raven.
His eyes are like doves,
Beside streams of water,
Bathed in milk,
And reposed in their setting.
His cheeks are like a bed of balsam,
Banks of sweet-scented herbs;
His lips are lilies,
Dripping with liquid myrrh.
His hands are rods of gold
Set with beryl;
His abdomen is carved ivory
Inlaid with sapphires.

Her remarks about his abdomen being carved in ivory seem to indicate that his stomach was firm. In other words, he wasn't suffering from "Dunlap's Disease"—*duh* belly *dun* lapped over *duh* belt!

Verbalizing uniqueness and excitement over your mate can't help but make him or her blossom as a person.

My wife has done something with me that I just cannot get over.

For some reason, ever since we've been married, Carol has told me that she likes my "bod." I've taken Carol with me to the mirror and we've even had her eyes checked by specialists, but she still says she likes my body. Let me make one thing clear—I've never been confused with any Mr. Universe contestants. I've even been told that I would never pass the first test in getting into one of those contests since the first thing they want is a picture. But Carol likes my body, and she tells me that often. It makes me feel incredible. Not only that, but it encourages me to find total satisfaction with Carol's body. Are you satisfied with your mate's body? More important, have you told him or her so? In the Song of Solomon, Shulamit and Solomon just keep telling each other how much they like each other's bodies. That kind of response will build a relationship up and encourage each partner to continue moving toward oneness.

The Song of Solomon also points out that the sexual relationship can be one of total freedom. Two people should feel free to enjoy anything in their sexual relationship, as long as it is in line with two principles: (1) it must meet your mate's needs; and (2) it must be done by mutual consent. There is nothing dirty about any part of the body or any kind of sexual act as long as it is done in line with these principles.

The final section of the Song of Solomon speaks of *sexual creativity*.

SHULAMIT: Why should you gaze at the Shulammite,
As at the dance of the two companies?

Shulamit is doing a little belly dance before Solomon (the "two companies" means the dance of the thighs!) and she is wondering why Solomon is staring at her (6:13)! Solomon has a typical male response (7:1–4):

SOLOMON: How beautiful are your feet in sandals,
O prince's daughter!
The curves of your hips are like jewels,

> The work of the hands of an artist.
> Your naval is like a round goblet
> Which never lacks mixed wine;
> Your belly is like a heap of wheat
> Fenced about with lilies.
> Your two breasts are like two fawns,
> Twins of a gazelle.
> Your neck is like a tower of ivory,
> Your eyes like the pools in Heshbon
> By the gate of Bath-rabbim;
> Your nose is like the tower of Lebanon,
> Which faces toward Damascus.

Something that gives me great encouragement in the Song of Solomon is that I don't think Shulamit and Solomon would have won any Miss America-Mr. Atlas awards. Yet each was totally ravished with the presence of the other and expressive of their love and commitment. They had a maximum marriage!

Solomon continues his praises over his wife (7:5–9):

> Your head crowns you like Carmel,
> And the flowing locks of your head are like purple
>   threads;
> The king is captivated by your tresses.
> How beautiful and how delightful you are,
> My love, with all your charms!
> Your stature is like a palm tree,
> And your breasts are like its clusters.
> I said, "I will climb the palm tree,
> I will take hold of its fruit stalks."
> Oh, may your breasts be like clusters of the vine,
> And the fragrance of your breath like apples,
> And your mouth like the best wine!

Here he goes again! Solomon is again praising Shulamit's body and expressing his sexual desire for her.

Sex, in order to be what it is designed to be, must be based on a committed love. In our society we don't know what love is. Somebody says, "I love oranges." What does he mean? He means that oranges do something for him and once he gets done squeezing everything out of that orange, he will discard it. Marital love is often viewed in the same way. Two people say, "I love you" to each other, but what they really mean is that the person does something for them and once they squeeze everything out of that person, they will discard him or her. That is not love! The love talked about in the Song of Solomon and in the biblical game plan for marriage is a love that says, "I love you, therefore I am committed to you. I want to give to you and seek your best."

That's what is so exciting about marriage! I know I have one person on my team, no matter what.

Sex Is a Priority That Takes Time

So take time! Solomon's late-night approach and the "ten-minute quickie" allow little time for enjoyment or communication.

Sex is not to be an afterthought but demands forethought. In our pressurized world a two-week vacation once a year is a meager relief from the stress and tension of life. Plan frequent getaways! They don't have to be expensive, but an extended time together can be extremely significant in building and maintaining a oneness factor in your marriage.

One word of caution: Prepare for distractions. For instance, you may want a lock on your bedroom door. If you have kids, you *will* want a lock on your bedroom door! The telephone may need to be unplugged or covered. We've found that a bean bag performs sufficient strangulation on a phone.

Take the Song of Solomon with you on your getaways. Read the song together—the husband can read Solomon's part and the wife can read Shulamit's. The first time you read through, just discuss what they're saying. The second reading might be the real thing—where you both are speaking your parts to each other. Now there is a third part in the song: it's the chorus. It's not really a chorus, but a literary device for changing scenes. So don't feel compelled to take ten or twelve people with you on your getaway.

As you read the song to each other, you'll be well on your way to making love by use of the Bible. That's biblical lovemaking! It's the most intimate expression of a maximum marriage—two people in a dynamic, intimate oneness, finding individual fulfillment through that oneness.

Part IV

The Supernatural Factor: Disorder or Design?

12

A Game Plan for Living Together

If it weren't for marriage, husbands and wives would have to fight with strangers! Marriage has become a battleground for using, bruising, and abusing everyone—men, women, and children. The problems created through marriage are marketed to society and the next generation. We all are affected by these problems because of the massive web of relationships in our world.

But no matter the damage and wreckage we have seen. Over 96 percent of our society keeps giving it another try. There's an urge to merge physically and psychologically that people are unable to shake. Thus far, I have suggested that the most healthy way to fill this inevitable urge to merge is by making three vital commitments:

1. the oneness factor
2. the responsibility factor
3. the intimacy factor

Although I am convinced through my counseling and personal experience that these three commitments work well, they are not enough. There is an underlying factor that upholds and even gives life to the other three. I call it the Supernatural Factor!

The supernatural factor battles against the two primary, intangible forces that eventually wear out a marriage. The first is that *relationships continue to fall apart.* Left to themselves, things go from bad to worse! The marital relationship is certainly not an exception. Marriages are falling apart right now. The only way to reverse this tendency of degeneration is to work very hard on your relationships. That's why the commitments (although simple and basic common sense) are so critical to creating a maximum marriage. It's the kind of hard work necessary to keep it together.

But there is something more that is added to a marriage—a new dimension—when there is a commitment to the supernatural factor. It's a commitment to a God consciousness—inviting God to be a part of your life and marriage. There is a *spiritual glue* that is applied to the marriage to help prevent the relationship from falling apart. This glue is obviously not a guarantee, but the amazing thing is that as long as people cultivate this commitment, the miraculous sticky glue seems to work! "The family that prays together, stays together," is not just a religious rumor, but a relevant reality!

The second primary negative force that the supernatural factor counteracts is the fact that *people continue to fail.* Contrary to popular opinion, when God invades a person's life, He doesn't come with a system of do's and don'ts to regulate your life. But when invited to be involved in a person's life, He comes with great amounts of forgiveness, grace, and healing. He is interested in *dissolving the guilt!* It doesn't take long for a guilt pile to accumulate in a marriage. Unless you deal with it, massive piles build up, hindering the kind of communication you desire and need for a marriage to be healthy.

The supernatural factor says that *God designed the family and only He can make it work best!* It's interesting to note that there are two foundational factors to every civilization: a God consciousness and family. When these two are destroyed, the civilization dies. In other words, every civilization has fallen when the Designer's design is broken. Since God designed the family, let Him help you make it work!

God is like the sun! When the sun shines its rays, it sheds light. I don't look at the sun and examine it. I could be blinded! I don't even know that much about it, but it's there and it is very helpful. God sends His rays of truth, His principles of life, that shed light on how life works best. You cannot look at Him, touch Him, or know everything about Him, but because His light rays make life work, you know He's there and ready to help!

The supernatural factor is the commitment that puts it all together. It dissolves the guilt and applies the glue to the marital relationship. Every marriage needs a miracle to keep it alive. The supernatural factor provides that miracle as the missing dynamic to a maximum marriage.

A maximum marriage is a dynamic, intimate, oneness through which a man and woman find their individual fulfillment. Your maximum marriage will not just happen—you must make it happen! Recently I read a statement that perfectly expresses what it takes to create your own maximum marriage:

Fewer marriages would skid if more who said "I do" did!

Source Notes

Chapter 5
1. This is taken from my book *Stress in the Family* (Eugene, Oregon: Harvest House Publishers, Inc., 1982).

Chapter 8
1. This is taken from my book *Loneliness Is Not a Disease* (Eugene, Oregon: Harvest House Publishers, Inc., 1981).
2. John Powell, *Why Am I Afraid to Tell You Who I Am?* (Allen, Texas: Argus Communications, 1969), chapter 3.
3. Ibid., pp. 56, 57.
4. John Powell, *Why Am I Afraid to Love?* (Allen, Texas: Argus Communications, 1972), pp. 100, 101.
5. John Powell, *The Secret of Staying in Love* (Allen, Texas: Argus Communications, 1974), p. 130.
6. Alan L. McGinnis, *The Friendship Factor* (Minneapolis: Augsburg Publishing House, 1979), p. 28.
7. Powell, *Secret*, p. 34.
8. Powell, *Why Am I Afraid to Tell You Who I Am?* p. 70.
9. Ibid., p. 74.
10. David Augsburger, *Caring Enough to Confront* (Ventura, California: Regal Books, 1980), p. 52.
11. David Augsburger, *The Freedom of Forgiveness* (Evanston, Illinois: Moody Press, 1970), p. 13.

12. Judson J. Swihart, *How Do You Say "I Love You"?* (Downers Grove, Illinois: Inter-Varsity Press, 1977), p. 55.
13. Dan Montgomery and Everett L. Shostrom, *Healing Love* (New York: Bantam Books, Inc., 1979), p. 87.
14. McGinnis, *Friendship*, p. 86.
15. Ibid., p. 89.
16. William Backus and Marie Chapian, *Telling Yourself the Truth* (Minneapolis: Bethany House Publishers, 1980), p. 142.
17. Powell, *Secret*, p. 13.